# Praise for *The Innovation Biome*

"*The Innovation Biome* is a must-read regardless of the stage of your career. Managers and leaders will gain new insights into methods and tools that unlock innovation in their organizations. Employees at every level will benefit from the wide range of inspiring success stories, and learn the elements necessary for achieving true breakthroughs."

—**JOHN CONNORS,** Board Director, Nike; Managing Partner, Ignition Ventures; Former CFO, Microsoft

"From Roger Bannister to the smallpox vaccine, Kumar Mehta will help you think deeply about innovation (and how you can find your breakthrough)."

—**SETH GODIN,** author of *Linchpin: Are You Indispensible?*

"An important book that lays out the foundational elements necessary for innovation and the steps required to making innovation a sustained activity for growth. A must-read for executives who want to build value through innovation."

—**NIRAV TOLIA,** CEO, Nextdoor

"*The Innovation Biome* concisely and coherently brings together a number of key themes on the topic of innovation and delivers a practical framework that leaders can apply."

—**BERT VALDMAN,** President and CEO, Optimum Energy

"When Kumar Mehta shared the ideas in this book with our team at HBS, it felt as if we were welcoming a new member to our group. He intrigued us with his concept of 'the next big thing' and then hooked us with his guiding focus on customer experience, and the concept of the 'experience delta.' Readers will sense his deep experience behind every page, as well as his deep passion to teach what he knows on this important subject."

—**DEREK VAN BEVER**, Director, Forum for Growth
and Innovation, Harvard Business School

"This is a rare pearl in a sea of books about innovation. This book builds on the science of innovation to provide organizations an essential guide to cultivating an enduring innovation biome that leads to sustained value creation."

—**JORDAN USDAN**, Senior Director, Corporate
Strategy & Development, Microsoft

"This is a very important book. There is no shortage of books, even very good ones, written on innovation, disruption and change written by business professors offering a prescription for success. Kumar Mehta's *The Innovation Biome* is so much more than that. It is written from the inside by a skilled innovator who has been an instrumental player at all levels of technology from major companies (Microsoft) to his own successful startups. It is filled with compelling examples and lessons that can only be learned by being in the middle of disruption, not by studying it. The reader immediately senses he is on a journey narrated by an expert in this confusing world of change. It will easily become a standard in business schools (and far more) replacing the books written by those schools' own faculty."

—**JEFFERY COLE**, PhD, Center for the Digital Future and Director of
the World Internet Project, University of Southern California

"As a global impact investor, we look at innovation broadly, from health-care to education to transportation. *The Innovation Biome* brings a unique historical perspective on the full spectrum of innovation that goes far beyond the typical understanding of venture capitalists. Kumar Mehta succinctly lays out the building blocks required for innovation. He provides a pragmatic roadmap for CEOs who want to foster an innovation culture that continuously delivers inspiring offerings for customers."

—**WILL POOLE,** Cofounder and Managing Partner, Capria Ventures; former Senior Vice President, Windows Client Business, Microsoft

"The concept of an 'Innovation Biome' is in itself exciting and yet, at the same time, so logical, so intuitive, so obviously right that you wonder why it has not already entered the innovation lexicon. Corporations—and organizations in general—so often get in their own way, and nowhere more so than in pursuing the golden goose of innovation. Here is a primer for every CEO for how to get out of his or her own way and let loose the creative impulses that already exist at every level in their organization. Read and learn!"

—**SIMON CHADWICK,** Managing Partner, Cambiar Consulting

# The
# Innovation
# BIOME

## A SUSTAINED BUSINESS ENVIRONMENT
## WHERE INNOVATION THRIVES

### KUMAR MEHTA, Ph.D.

RIVER GROVE
BOOKS

Published by River Grove Books
Austin, TX
www.rivergrovebooks.com

Distributed by River Grove Books

Design and composition by Greenleaf Book Group
Cover design by Greenleaf Book Group
Cover images © ExpressVectors, 2012. Used under license from Shutterstock.com;
©iStockphoto.com/Robert_Ford

Cataloging-in-Publication data is available.

Print ISBN: 978-1-63299-156-0

eBook ISBN: 978-1-63299-157-7

First Edition

*For Palvi, Curren, and Priyanka.*

# Contents

# Preface

A recent search on the term *innovation* on Amazon.com yielded over seventy thousand books and articles available for sale, and a Google search on the term *innovation strategy* yielded a few million results. A lot has already been written on this topic. Plus, there are innumerable consultants, innovation experts, practitioners, academics, researchers, and advisors, all with well-thought-out theories, observations, and perspectives—ideas and strategies we can all learn from.

So why one more book?

Despite everything written about innovation (or maybe *because* of everything written about innovation), there is still no clear view on what innovation is and how companies can become more innovative. And as important as innovation is to the continued success and very existence of a corporation, the process of innovation is a jumbled mess, with multiple and sometimes conflicting theories. Countless books and articles promote a specific methodology or the hot new tool or approach, which soon goes out of favor to be replaced by another hot new approach. Even the definition and basic taxonomy of innovation vary, and there is no consensus on how to measure it. If any other corporate process, such as finance, operations, manufacturing, or sales, had the same level of ambiguity, uncertainty, and unaccountability as the innovation process has, a business could hardly be run with any degree of effectiveness. It is not surprising that companies are getting little return from their investments in innovation.

## Are you doing it wrong or developing it right?

A plethora of strategies and techniques designed to spur innovation have always been available. These days, some of the current tools that are supposed to transform a slow-growth company into an innovation-driven market leader may include the following:

- Sending executives to Silicon Valley to learn the secrets of innovation
- Applying lean techniques and rapid prototyping
- Applying data science and predictive analytics
- Adopting an open-innovation platform
- Building an internal startup
- Adopting a fast-trial and fast-failure approach

- Building an office environment that provides the illusion of supporting innovative thinking
- Acquiring a hot and promising startup

While all of these techniques have merit, we can safely assume that if there were a single solution that made companies innovative, we would have known about it by now, and everyone would have adopted it. The simple fact is that the only way to become innovative is to understand what drives innovation and to establish conditions that let the drivers of innovation thrive.

Establishing the conditions that encourage innovation is the best way for your company to consciously develop an environment that consistently lets you produce offerings with new and novel value—innovations in the eyes of your users. The most innovative companies do this instinctively—perhaps because of the culture instilled by superstar leaders, a conscious and successful effort, or the emergence of the right conditions after things just fell into place. But the fact is that every company can develop this innate innovation capability—an *innovation biome*—and in this book, I set out to explain how.

## The innovation biome

A natural *biome* is a specific environment that provides the macro conditions where a certain system of life exists. The biome provides the settings or conditions that determine what flourishes and what dies. An innovation biome is a corporate environment that lets innovation flourish. It requires a set of conditions to nurture it and allow it to propagate. Without the right biome, innovation efforts will undoubtedly fail.

An innovation biome is built on the foundational knowledge of what drives innovation. There are no tools to buy, no one-size-fits-all methodologies to adopt, no software platforms to deploy, and no quick-fix solutions to implement. A healthy biome requires that you and your organization understand that innovation is an ongoing process that will outlive every tool and methodology. The only way to realize the vision of innovation is by understanding and adopting the common principles of innovation that have worked well for thousands of years. They will work well for thousands more, but you must evolve your organization to ensure their presence. Just as the natural biome is established and evolves in a way that allows organic and natural breakthroughs to occur, the innovation biome provides the conditions that allow organizational breakthroughs to occur.

## How this book can help you

My approach to writing this book included a study of many of the greatest innovations in history, starting from the invention of the wheel over three thousand years ago to the world-changing developments we use and enjoy today, including the Internet, smartphones, contact lenses, robotic surgery, and many other innovative developments in between. My goal was to understand the building blocks of the innovation process. In essence, I was searching for the first principles, the basic truths and attributes that exist across all great creations. If we can understand the principles and attributes that drive innovation, we should be able to build conditions that let these attributes thrive. And in the presence of these conditions, the rate of innovation should increase.

The attributes, presented in part 2 of this book, represent the foundational building blocks that need to exist for any company trying to solve the innovation puzzle. In part 3, I'll share a taxonomy of innovation activities and a framework that can be applied within your company so that your innovation biome can flourish.

Everything in this book is based on research and the study of best practices not only from the field of innovation science but also from the social sciences, management science, improvement science, and the science behind creativity. Where possible, I have taken lessons learned and best practices from existing research in other disciplines and incorporated them into my approach to creating a successful innovation biome.

Cultivating an innovation biome requires taking specific actions, not just as a one-time initiative but as an ongoing discipline. It requires implementing strategies and methods that will enable and catalyze the innovation process. Most companies today already have systems for innovation in place; unfortunately, these systems usually do not yield the intended results. Companies often adopt new techniques that are the "flavor of the day," and if these approaches don't work, they quickly move on to the next. Additionally, each innovation technique is often deployed as a stand-alone solution. Innovation does not work that way. It must be a philosophy ingrained into the company's core. The creation of new and original value requires a lot of things to happen that are both within and outside a company's control.

The frameworks presented in this book are designed to help companies identify and use the right set of tools for the matching set of innovation activities. One of the common misconceptions today in the field of innovation study is that while most experts agree there are different classes of innovation, they still promote a single set of tools. One of the reasons innovation activities fail is because the tools that are best for a certain type of innovation are applied to something else, leading to a mismatch that impedes innovation.

For example, we will learn that applying data science and analytics are great for advancing and improving your current processes but not for the creation of new breakthroughs and transformations. A large, consolidated team is better for certain kinds of innovation activities, whereas smaller, disparate teams working independently are better for other types of innovation. This book shares a taxonomy of innovation activities and presents the right set of tools required for each type of innovation outcome.

## The innovation organization

Most organizations are not getting the innovation results they desire, but not from a lack of trying. In fact, it is likely the opposite: Perhaps they are trying too hard and spinning their wheels in the process. Every organization, large and small, understands the importance of innovation and wants to launch the next big thing. But as we will see, the next big thing is often a fallacy, and its pursuit rarely leads to innovation.

Similarly, many organizations go about other aspects of the innovation process erroneously, such as generating ideas or staffing innovation teams, leading to dissatisfactory results. This is because organizations don't have a deep understanding of innovation. We know that innovation is an extremely complex and unstructured endeavor that is influenced by an almost infinite number of internal and external variables. The best we can do to develop a sustainable innovation environment is to understand the foundational elements of innovation, ensure they are understood by the entire organization, and continually strive to establish the presence of these elements and stay true to them. If we achieve this, we will have an innovation biome.

The good news is that once the principles of innovation are woven into the fabric of an organization, the process of innovation becomes sustained and independent of any individual or technique. Only then can innovation become institutionalized; your organization can attain the elite and enviable level of sustained value creation and gain the rewards that go along with being a company that releases one great innovation after another.

When I started writing this book, I did not have a specific outcome or innovation theory in mind that I wanted to promote. The thoughts and outcomes presented in this book have emerged from the research I have done on innovation. Much like the process of innovation, the outcome and innovation models presented in these pages are a natural extension of some outstanding work done by experts in many fields and can simply be summarized as ideas building on other ideas.

Will you become more innovative after reading this book? There are too many variables involved in innovation to know, and one book is likely not going to change you overnight. But the reasoning presented here should get you started on the right journey. No one can guarantee that any single approach is going to make you an innovation juggernaut (and if anyone does, turn the other way), but creating a sustained environment that supports innovation—an innovation biome—is the first step.

# PART 1

---

## WHAT IS INNOVATION?

**On a windy day in May 1954, one** of the biggest barriers in sports, a feat that was considered by many as physiologically unattainable, was broken at Oxford University's Iffley Road track. Roger Bannister, a medical student, ran a mile in under four minutes for the first time on record.

A gifted runner, Bannister participated in the 1952 Olympics in Helsinki but returned home after a lackluster performance. Once he was back in England, he set a new goal. He wanted to be the first human to run a mile in under four minutes, the most coveted goal by middle-distance runners. Many were chasing this elusive goal, and a few elite runners were even closing in, but it appeared to always be just out of reach.

Bannister started to prepare. He established an unconventional and atypical training routine that included more rest days and harder running intervals on the days he did run. He learned techniques from the Swedish running greats of the time, Gunder Hägg and Arne Andersson. The Swedes used a training method called *fartlek* (speed play), a technique that mixes hard runs, easy runs, hill runs, and sprints almost randomly and with no fixed regimen. Each interval is different from the other.

Bannister believed in his heart that the four-minute-mile barrier could be broken. He believed he needed to split up the entire 1,600-meter distance into four separate 400-meter races (four laps) and run each one in under a minute in order to achieve his goal. During his training, he learned through trial and error that rest days gave him stronger legs and that harder intervals better prepared his body for the race.

Bannister even planned out his running environment to optimize for the environmental factors he considered instrumental to breaking the four-minute mile: the right track, no wind, and reasonably warm weather. He trained with his two talented pacemakers under the watchful eye of his Austrian coach, Franz Stampfl.

Finally, race day came. After five days of rest, Bannister was ready for the run. However, as is the case with almost every breakthrough, things didn't go according to plan, and Bannister had to work through the obstacles. It turned out to be a blustery day. Bannister almost pulled out, thinking that the conditions were not right for his attempt and that he should conserve his energy for another time. Bannister did not think he would reach his goal under these conditions, as he would have to run the equivalent of a sub-3.56-minute mile to overcome the negative effect of the wind. On the other hand, he thought that if he passed up this opportunity, he might never get another chance where his body, mind, partners—and even the crowd waiting for him—were so perfectly primed for the race.

Shortly before the race, Bannister decided to have a go at it. Aided by his two training partners and pacemakers, he ran the first of the four laps in 57.5 seconds. He crossed the halfway point in 1 minute 58 seconds. The third lap was slower, at a couple of seconds over a minute, and he needed to break the one-minute mark for the final lap.

The difference between a very good runner and an elite runner is the kick, the ability to increase your finishing speed to a whole new level of sprint. Either you have it, or you don't. Bannister did, and he ran the final lap in just under 59 seconds.

A month and a half after Bannister achieved this goal, his time was eclipsed by Australian runner John Landy. Soon, many other runners joined in breaking the four-minute-mile barrier.

There is no doubt that Roger Bannister's achievement was a breakthrough. This brief account of his story contains all the elements of creating breakthroughs in any endeavor. It has the primed-and-prepared mind and body of Roger Bannister. It has disbelief and skepticism from the community. It happened only because of a network of knowledge transfer and improvement processes, and an interconnected system that included his coach and two outstanding pacemakers working together. The timing and environment was just right, notwithstanding the sudden hiccup in weather. Once this milestone was achieved, it became easier for others to do the same. And like many other great innovations, if it hadn't been Bannister, someone else would have achieved it for all the same reasons.

While breaking a sports record may not be considered a world-altering innovation by some, the invention of vaccination certainly would be. Vaccination first eliminated the scourge of smallpox and, over time, eradicated many more diseases, saving millions of lives. Like Bannister's story, the discovery of vaccination typifies how great innovations are created. This story includes almost the same set of attributes as breaking the four-minute mile.

Over the centuries, smallpox had been the cause of major epidemics that devastated civilizations, including plagues that accounted for the deaths of millions of people around the world. In eighteenth-century Europe, four hundred thousand people died annually of smallpox, a third of the survivors went blind, and many more were left with disfiguring scars.

For over two thousand years, survivors of smallpox were known to be immune to the disease and were called on to take care of the afflicted. Over the centuries, physicians attempted to cure smallpox with a wide array of treatments, including my personal favorite: the administration of twelve small bottles of beer every twenty-four hours. In time, physicians learned that the most effective way of combating smallpox was through the administration of a small amount of the virus to the nonimmune population—the people who had not yet been exposed to the disease. This practice was developed simultaneously and independently by different researchers in different countries.

The process of attempting to protect someone from smallpox by injecting a small quantity of the virus itself was known as *variolation*. Variolation was sometimes effective, but it was fraught with risks. The most obvious risks were that the subjects could get smallpox and suffer the same fate as people contracting the disease naturally, or that other damaging diseases, such as syphilis, could be inadvertently transmitted in the process. However, compared to the beer-consumption therapy and other similar treatments, variolation was by and large a successful approach to slowing down the spread of smallpox. In fact, during the small-pox epidemic of 1721 in Boston, where approximately half the citizens were exposed to smallpox, doctors observed that while the mortality rate of people who contracted smallpox was 14 percent, those who were variolated had a mortality rate of 2 percent, a miraculous improvement. In contrast, vaccination, later developed by Edward Jenner, had a mortality rate of only one or two people in a million and was responsible for eliminating smallpox from the world.

During the late 1700s, Edward Jenner, who treated patients in the English countryside, observed a common phenomenon: Milk-maids were immune to smallpox. This was because they worked with cows all day long and had likely been exposed to cowpox, a disease less harmful than, but related to, smallpox. In fact, Jenner overheard a milkmaid say, "I shall never have smallpox, for I have had cowpox. I shall never have an ugly, pockmarked face."[1] Jenner surmised that cowpox not only protected people against smallpox but could be transmitted from one to another as a deliberate mechanism of protection.

In 1796, he found a dairymaid with fresh cowpox lesions on her hands. Using the substance from the lesions, he injected an eight-year-old boy with cowpox. After an initial mild fever and discomfort, the boy felt better, and Jenner then injected him with the matter from a fresh smallpox lesion. No disease developed.

---

1    Stefan Riedel, MD, PhD, "Edward Jenner and the History of Smallpox and Vaccination," *Proceedings of the Baylor University Medical Center*, vol. 18 (2005): 21–25, https://www.ncbi.nlm.nih.gov/pmc/articles/PMC1200696/.

Jenner concluded that the experiment worked and, in 1797, wrote up his findings for publication, but his paper was rejected. The following year, he added a few more successful case studies documenting the use of the less harmful cowpox to prevent one of the deadliest-known diseases of the time and published a booklet on his findings. He called his process *vaccination* (from *vaccinia*, the Latin term for cowpox). This publication was met with mixed reaction.

Next, Jenner went to London to look for volunteers for vaccination. After three months, he had found none. No one believed him. Inoculating someone with something taken from a diseased animal was considered hideous and blasphemous.

Eventually, another surgeon, to whom Jenner had given some of his inoculum, tried out his technique. In 1799, a few more surgeons began supporting vaccination. Then, suddenly, vaccination took off. Within a year of the turn of the century, this technique was being used in most European countries. Jenner was the hero, the innovator who had found a cure to one of the world's deadliest diseases. Over time, his method was used to fight new diseases like polio, whooping cough, measles, and tetanus.

While Jenner gave scientific credence to vaccination, he was not the first to vaccinate using cowpox. Twenty years earlier, a farmer in England by the name of Benjamin Jesty had successfully used a similar technique. Jesty was determined to protect his family from smallpox, and after taking some pustular material from a cow's udder, he used a darning needle to transfer the material by scratching the arms of his family. He was labeled as inhuman and physically attacked by his neighbors, as the thought of transmitting an animal's disease into a human was considered repulsive. His wife and two sons, who were exposed to smallpox, never caught the disease.

Jesty's story, not nearly as famous as Jenner's, simply goes to show that if Jenner had not made his discovery, the concept of vaccination would have still been alive—and perhaps a little-known farmer who simply loved and protected his family would have been the hero.

The story of vaccination, like the one of Roger Bannister, also prominently features individual innovators being primed for a discovery. Their invention faced resistance and disbelief based on conventional wisdom. Simultaneous developments were under way by other innovators, and an interconnected network of knowledge transfer was crucial. A period of slow initial acceptance was followed by the rapid adoption of the innovation as soon as knowledge of the breakthrough was available. The innovation took place in the right environment—during an age in which science was gaining prominence and the underlying processes of disease transmission were nearly understandable. Finally, a cluster of value was created to distribute the vaccine to the population, including trained personnel to administer the virus.

This book is about the elements that create breakthrough innovations. It is about the factors that influence innovation. If we can clearly identify and understand the attributes that help and hamper the creation of breakthrough innovations, we can develop conditions that allow these attributes to exist and thrive. And in the presence of these conditions, the process of innovation can result in an accelerated rate of creation of breakthroughs. Simply by establishing the presence of the right conditions, we can, in effect, institutionalize the process of innovation.

## Big business innovation

In 2016, the top one thousand corporations spent $680 billion in R&D.[2] If you add to this figure what the rest of the world spends on R&D, it's safe to assume that we spend a trillion (yes, with a *t*) dollars on R&D every single year. This is a staggering sum. What do we have to show for it?

In 2016, Greg Ip proclaimed in *The Wall Street Journal*[3] that we are in an innovation paradox. He suggested that we appear to be advancing in fields such as artificial intelligence (AI), gene therapy, and robotics. However, except for technology, our lives are the same as they were a few decades ago. Houses haven't evolved beyond a slightly smarter thermostat, flight travel is no faster—and certainly no better (though it is safer)—than it was twenty years ago, and the twenty most prescribed drugs in the US were all introduced over a decade ago. Furthermore, Ip stated that innovation's contribution to economic growth peaked at 3.4 percent per year in the 1950s but has dropped to a disappointing 0.5 percent over the past decade.

There is no reason for the rate of corporate innovation to be this slow. Corporations have the smartest and best-compensated executives and managers. They have world-class researchers, with access to virtually every piece of available information. They have the largest resources and the blessing of shareholders who approve massive R&D budgets. They have the brand and the marketing muscle, as

---

2    PwC, "2016 Global Innovation Report," PwC Strategy& website, https://www. strategyand.pwc.com/innovation1000.

3    Greg Ip, "The Economy's Hidden Problem: We're Out of Big Ideas," *Wall Street Journal* (December 20, 2016), https://www.wsj.com/articles/the-economys -hidden-problem-were-out-of-big-ideas-1481042066.

well as the ability, to get innovations out into society far faster than an unknown startup can. Plus, these are the organizations that want to be and claim to be innovative. Yet the development of transformative products frequently eludes these companies.

To be clear, the trillion-dollar R&D expenditure is certainly effective in creating many new ideas. In fact, over 325,000 patents were granted in 2015 alone, and millions more have been granted over the past decade. Many of these were granted to corporations, with companies like IBM, Samsung, Canon, Qualcomm, Google, Toshiba, Sony, LG, Intel, and Microsoft leading the way. These R&D efforts create thousands of novel ideas every day, and I would bet that corporations are already in the middle of potentially world-changing developments. But something gets in the way. Many of these ideas and patents don't become marketable products for any number of reasons, and an unfortunate consequence is that the overall rate of innovation for the organization— as well as for society—suffers.

Large corporations, in their current forms, are often not designed to be innovative. There are many well-documented reasons for this. One of the most popular theories is disruptive innovation, a well-known and well-documented concept introduced by Clayton Christensen and Joseph Bower in 1995,[4] where companies focus on product improvements designed to serve their most profitable customers. In doing so, they often miss out on the disruptive forces that can shrink large markets or make them entirely irrelevant.

---

4    Joseph L. Bower and Clayton M. Christensen, "Disruptive Technologies: Catching the Wave," *Harvard Business Review* (January–February 1995), https://hbr.org/1995/01/disruptive-technologies-catching-the-wave.

Take Kodak, for example. Here is a company that did everything it was supposed to in order to support its highly profitable franchise (selling rolls of film) but was displaced by a world in which everyone uses a digital camera. The ubiquity of cameras should have been the biggest of booms for the leader in the photography business, as there are orders of magnitude more photos being taken and shared today than ever before. However, the sad reality is that Kodak had to file for bankruptcy in 2012.

A lot of people may not know this, but the original digital camera was, in fact, developed at Kodak by a bright young engineer named Steven Sasson in 1975. However, at the time, the company did not see this innovation fitting in to the existing profitable business model, so it was deprioritized. While Kodak did profit from the digital wave through the patents it held, one of its own great inventions caused the downfall of one of the greatest brands in history.

This is not Kodak's fault; it did everything right, according to the textbook: it focused on its high-growth, high-margin business. Back in the 1970s, the images from these newfangled electronic cameras that did not use film or paper were unrefined. The process was clunky, and while the engineer behind this technology may have seen the promise, the company did not.[5]

Kodak is hardly alone; there are countless examples of groundbreaking ideas or technologies that never see the light of day. In some cases, they never rise to the right level of attention, or sometimes the

---

5    James Estrin, "Kodak's First Digital Moments," *New York Times* (August 12, 2015), https://lens.blogs.nytimes.com/2015/08/12/kodaks-first-digital-moment.

most profitable product line is given more deference, which often prevents other great ideas and technologies from coming to fruition.

As most readers may know, Steve Jobs first learned about the computer mouse and the graphical user interface in 1979 from Xerox PARC, the innovation center for Xerox Corporation. It had a great creation in the original mouse, which was designed to control activities on a computer screen.[6] However, as we well know today, it was Jobs and Apple (not Xerox) who made the concept of the computer mouse ubiquitous and created immense societal and shareholder value from this invention. In fact, years later Jobs said, "If Xerox had known what it had and had taken advantage of its real opportunities, it could have been as big as IBM plus Microsoft plus Xerox combined—and the largest high-technology company in the world."[7]

Today, many large companies already have in their possession, like Kodak and Xerox did, great ideas and developments. They have either developed or are in the process of developing their own version of the next digital camera or the next mouse. As we saw earlier, the trillions spent on R&D have resulted in many patentable inventions. However, the challenge is in identifying which of them to bet on and in allowing them to blossom and fulfill their potential.

Enhancing the rate of innovation in a large organization involves thinking differently about management, rewards, failure,

---

6    The computer mouse was actually invented earlier by Douglas Engelbart at the Stanford Research Institute, who has also developed some theoretical models on innovation that we will address later in the book.

7    Malcolm Gladwell, "Creation Myth," *New Yorker* (May 16, 2011), http://www.newyorker.com/magazine/2011/05/16/creation-myth.

risk taking, priorities, placement of the best and brightest people, and the innovation process in general. Entrepreneurs have an intrinsic understanding of how to think innovatively. Corporations have lost that somewhere along the line.

This is not because corporations lack entrepreneurial talent. They have within their ranks the bold thinkers and entrepreneurs who can take the great ideas and build successful businesses from them. Studies have shown that corporations are the greatest breeding ground for entrepreneurs. The Kauffman Foundation studied 549 founders of successful businesses in high-growth industries, including aerospace, defense, computing, electronics, and health care.[8] Their study shows that over 75 percent of these successful entrepreneurs worked at other companies for more than six years before starting their own companies, and, unlike the vision we may hold in our minds of successful entrepreneurs, the average age of these company founders was forty. I am a living example of this phenomenon. After more than thirteen years, I left a large organization, Microsoft, and started and managed several successful companies. My large-company experience trained me to be an entrepreneur, and everything I know about how to manage and grow a company I learned at Microsoft.

The problem is that corporations are unable to retain the entrepreneurs within their ranks. The most creative and motivated talent goes off to start new companies that often create immense societal (and shareholder) value against all odds. Had the original

---

8    Ewing Marion Kauffman Foundation, "The Anatomy of an Entrepreneur," Kauffman website (July 9, 2009), http://www.kauffman.org/what-we-do/ research/2010/05/the-anatomy-of-an-entrepreneur.

employers been able to provide a more fertile environment for innovation, there is a good chance that great new business ventures would have been formed internally. And since these innovations would have been supported by the resources of a large organization, their chances of success would have been greater (many experts estimate that 80–90 percent of startups fail).

Innovation can become a core competency. It can be institutionalized within your company and become an ongoing, replicable, and measurable activity that creates substantial societal and shareholder value. This book shares the common elements that exist across all great developments that you can apply. It also contains frameworks that you can implement to create value through innovation.

## The science of innovation

Science is the constant that has led to the deep understanding we have of the physical world and the social world, and it has been the foundation of most of the greatest inventions in history. The science of innovation is more social than physical. In physical science, if you replicate the conditions of any scientific principle, the exact same results are expected. In innovation science, that is simply not possible; there are innumerable factors that drive the creation of new value. Instead we are studying patterns in human behavior and applying the knowledge gained to benefit humanity.

Innovation is the lifeblood of humanity. Without innovation, we would still be living in caves (though finding the first cave to live in was quite an innovation at the time). Today, almost every successful corporation in the world is founded on bringing an innovative concept to customers, but as the company becomes a large enterprise, that innovative edge is often lost. Corporations are continually trying to recreate that edge and rekindle that innovative spirit. However, the truth is that most life-changing innovations come from the startup world or from genius leaders (think Thomas Edison, Steve Jobs, Bill Gates, and Elon Musk) who, with a firm vision, push innovations through a large and complex enterprise.

It doesn't have to be that way. Innovation is not—and should not be—limited to genius inventors or startups who doggedly pursue a vision. Large corporations can also innovate at a vastly accelerated pace, especially given the hundreds of billions of dollars they spend every year in R&D capabilities to spur innovation. Yet few great ideas and concepts created by large corporations are developed for commercial release, let alone become world-changing successes.

In this book we'll discuss a set of research-supported principles for how large corporations can revive the innovation forces that made them who they are in the first place. I'll draw on lessons learned from the greatest innovations in history. There are common themes that can be applied by any company trying to be innovative. I'll also introduce the concept of *experiential innovation*, an activity that is missing in many companies. This form of innovation, which involves using available knowledge and techniques to build new experiences, has led to many of the greatest innovations society has enjoyed. With the right understanding, we can implement approaches to make this a core competency of an organization. Finally, I'll detail the tools, techniques, and thought processes required to innovate for experience enhancement, as that is what every single innovation does.

One of the things I emphasize throughout the book is that innovation is not about the value in creating ideas; it is about the ideas creating value.

# CHAPTER 1

# Types of Innovation

**We all know something is innovative when we** see it and touch it for the first time. The first time I held an iPhone in my hand, I thought it was the greatest piece of engineering ever created. Remember, it was released in 2007, when tech-savvy people were using the triple-tap technique on a cramped keypad, most likely a flip phone or a Blackberry, to uncover the limited amount of information you could access from your mobile device at the time.

The concept of a phone with a touch screen, a full web browser, and the ability to pinch and expand and tilt seemed like a mind-blowing idea to me at the time. Now, for most of us, the novelty of the iPhone has worn off, and it is a utility device that we use every day—even though the value it provides increases each day and with each new app. However, everyone would agree that this is an innovation that remarkably changed how we live, access information, and communicate.

So, while we don't need to define an innovation—since we know one when we see one—I would like to start by framing the concept of innovation with my favorite definition (out of the countless definitions out there). The US Patent and Trademark Office describes *innovation* as a process or "a series of steps that begins with human imagination and creativity and results in the creation of something of value for society to enjoy. Innovation is not defined by just a single event or even a single brilliant idea. The creation of intellectual property takes vision and perseverance and often involves people from different backgrounds and expertise collaborating in order to transform an idea into something that is real and tangible."[9]

One of the reasons innovating is difficult is that it has been classified in countless ways, and people think about it in different ways. Sometimes innovations are described as any of these terms:

- Product innovations

- Process innovations

- Service innovations

- Platform innovations

- Business model innovations

- Frugal innovations

- Radical innovations

---

9   US Patent and Trademark Office, "Innovation Overview" (2017), https://www.uspto.gov/learning-and-resources/outreach-and-education/science-innovation-video-series#overview.

- Open innovations
- Architectural innovations
- Design innovations
- Disruptive innovations
- Breakthrough innovations

And there are many other forms of innovation. In fact, probably more than a hundred types of innovations have been published.

It is important to have a clear and lucid view regarding the types of innovation, because different types of innovation require different activities and tools. Using a set of tools for one type of innovation that is designed for another set of activities is a waste of time, money, and effort, and promises to be a frustrating process.

Three types of innovation create most of the societal value, and they are the focus of this book:

- Incremental innovation
- Breakthrough innovation
- Transformational or experiential innovation

The first of these, *incremental* innovation, includes improvements to offerings that are already available in your organization. This type often generates the next version of or improvements to your product. It may include logical extensions to products and services, improvements in design or manufacture, usability improvements, or ways to reach more customers. The next version of a smartphone, next year's model of an automobile, the next generation of a razor (e.g., adding another blade), a localized version of software, and a better formulation of a drug are all incremental innovations.

*Breakthrough* innovation includes brand-new creations without a precedent. This is a new discovery or invention with the potential to significantly enhance lives, often through the advancement of science and technology. This type includes most of the innovative discoveries developed through original R&D, such as penicillin, the Internet, the automobile, and the airplane.

*Transformational* or *experiential* innovations create new experiences. They may not be brand-new inventions; instead they repurpose existing inventions and functionality to create new experiences. Examples include commercial aviation (not the invention of the airplane itself, but the use of airplanes to transport millions of people every day), online shopping (again, not the Internet but its use as the world's largest shopping mall), the iPhone, and Uber. Each of these offerings transformed the lives of millions by synthesizing existing (already invented) capabilities and technology to achieve the transformation.

These types of innovation are fairly easy to identify, but the crucial point—and what many companies fail to realize—is that each of these categories requires a certain set of activities. The wrong activities will not only hinder your innovation efforts but may actually damage them. The correct pairing, though, is what will allow your company's innovation biome to flourish. We'll discuss these pairings at length later in the book, but for now, let's get back to basics.

# CHAPTER 2

# First-Principles Innovation

**People love their burgers. Americans consume close to** ten billion burgers every year, making it the most popular food in the country. People love the texture, the taste, the aromas, the emotional appeal, and the feeling that comes from every juicy bite they chew. However, burgers are not good for the planet.

Plant-based burgers have been widely available for a long time and in many varieties, but they have always remained a niche and been consumed almost exclusively by vegetarians. Meat lovers, the vast majority of burger consumers, have found these plant-based versions lacking in many of the attributes they desire and crave and have consequently never warmed up to them. Environmentally, the problem with burgers and meat-based food is that the required livestock and production process consume a lot of resources. There is simply too much inefficiency when a cow or chicken on a vegetarian diet gets converted into a protein-rich food source for humans. Animal agriculture uses around 30 percent of all land and a third of all fresh water on the planet and creates as much greenhouse gas as all cars, trucks, trains, ships, and airplanes combined.[10]

Enter Impossible Foods, a company that decided to make a burger entirely from plant-based resources without compromising on any of the attributes that are so endearing to meat lovers. In effect, it attempted to recreate in a lab every appealing aspect of the burger while using (according to their estimates) 95 percent less land and 74 percent less water, as well as emitting 87 percent less greenhouse gases.

It achieved its mission by disintegrating the traditional burger to the molecular level, understanding the makeup of every component, and then diligently finding the right plant-based materials to create a new burger with the same sensory attributes. Although the Impossible Burger is not made of beef, at the root level all of the flavors, textures, tastes, and smells are designed to be the same as a beef burger's.

This decomposition of the burger into its most fundamental and basic root attributes is akin to *first-principles* reasoning, in which a topic is disintegrated or deconstructed in the same way.

---

10  Bryan Walsh, "The Triple Whopper Environmental Impact of Global Meat Production," *Time* (December 16, 2013), http://science.time.com/2013/12/16/the-triple-whopper-environmental-impact-of-global-meat-production.

Huffington Post, "Animal Agriculture's Impact on Climate Change," Climate Nexus (2015), http://climatenexus.org/learn/food/animal-agriculture%E2%80%99s-impact-climate-change.

First-principles thinking was used by Aristotle over twenty-five hundred years ago and involves breaking down an argument or an assumption into its most basic truths or undeniable principles.[11] A first principle is a "basic, foundational, self-evident proposition or assumption"[12] that cannot be deduced from any other proposition or assumption. They are universal principles that all knowledge and science is built on.

Using the Impossible Foods burger as an example, the thinking is that if we can break down and isolate every single component of a meat-based burger into its most basic and elemental form, find the exact same individual components from other sources, and then put them all together in the same proportions, we should be able to recreate the qualities of the original burger using only environmentally friendly components. Only time will tell if the Impossible Burger is a first-principles innovation that will disrupt the multibillion-dollar hamburger industry, but it has had largely positive reviews and has been successful in raising over $180 million from investors who share in the vision. And since these burgers are designed in a lab, they are always getting better, and there is virtually no limit to how good they can get. For example, they can always adapt to changing tastes and preferences, something beef burgers cannot do.

Elon Musk, the celebrated and successful innovator and founder of PayPal, SpaceX, and Tesla, shared in an interview how

---

11  Aristotle, *Physics*, trans. R. P. Hardie and R. K. Gaye, The Internet Classics Archive, MIT (2000), http://classics.mit.edu/Aristotle/physics.mb.txt.

12  Wikipedia, "First principle" (2017), https://en.wikipedia.org/wiki/First_principle.

he uses first-principles thinking.[13] People normally reason by analogy, Musk said. But first principles let us see beyond common expectations. He described a simple example: the battery. Rather than simply accepting that batteries are expensive and that this cannot change, in a first-principles approach a company would break down a battery into its core materials—things like nickel, aluminum, and carbon, all inexpensive components. If the materials that make up a battery were bought separately and combined ingeniously in the shape of a battery, its total cost can be orders of magnitude cheaper, giving rise to endless new possible uses.

This is an excellent example of how first-principles thinking can drive innovation in ways that conventional thinking will never allow. You are able to rise to a higher level of abstraction and develop more creative solutions by narrowing the focus to understand the basic, necessary, and unalterable truths. First-principles reasoning can apply to any application or industry, because it provides a level of clarity that is not possible using any other method of thinking or reasoning. It brings into question every assumption we take for granted.

This book is an application of first-principles reasoning. I've attempted to break innovation down into its most basic building blocks and components. Since innovation is a complex and inexact process driven by countless individual factors, it is not possible (at least not yet) to have a concrete set of components, along with their individual contributions, that can be isolated and recreated

---

13   Kevin Rose, "The First Principles Method Explained by Elon Musk," Innomind interview (December 4, 2013) https://www.youtube.com/watch?v=NV3sBlRgzTI.

like the Impossible Burger. However, we'll discuss many of the core elements of innovation that I consider foundational. If other researchers and authors went through the same exercise that I did, they would likely come up with a similar or slightly different set of foundational components. If you are looking to build your innovation capability to produce more innovations more frequently, the principles presented in this book are a good place to start.

Your own innovation journey can start with first principles. Strip your product or offering down to its most basic and essential components. Question why each component is present, whether it really needs to be there, whether it can be replaced, and whether the components can be configured differently. Ask how every piece is contributing to the customer experience. Question every assumption. Assumptions that were made a long time ago may not hold true today. If you started creating your product from first-principles components rather than from existing product versions, could you develop something that is cheaper or more valuable to users?

First-principles reasoning works for any product or service. Take, for example, the case of an everyday product like cough syrup. Your basic components might be a cough suppressant, a pain reliever, a decongestant, and some flavoring, as well as alcohol to help dissolve the other ingredients. Alcohol is cheap, but some customers would prefer to avoid it. The cough suppressant is not water soluble, but your pain reliever and decongestant are. You can remove the alcohol if you replace the cough suppressant with a different formula. You can also save some expense if you remove the decongestant and focus on the core goal of reducing pain and discomfort from coughing rather than the general symptoms of a cold or flu virus. You might think that cough syrup must be cherry flavored or have that cloying, nondescript medicine taste, but if there is no reason behind the choice, why not use something more exotic—say, fig flavoring. Now, maybe you add in some caffeine so that the user feels awake rather than groggy. Finally, if you exchange your chemical suppressant and pain reliever for natural plant ingredients that perform the same function, you've created a new market: a natural cough syrup that is alcohol free, provides an energy boost, tastes good, is less expensive, and is likely different from everything else out there. Simply by questioning and rethinking some assumptions and reconfiguring components, you could have a new product that enhances the customer experience; as an added benefit, the production costs might decrease, and you could have a fresh offering that is in line with today's tastes and not yesterday's assumptions.

This is a valuable exercise to engage in periodically during a product cycle so that you are not caught up in doing things a certain way because they have always been done that way. This is the type of thinking that creates new value. In the cough syrup example, the resulting changes could result in incremental (yet valuable) innovation. In other cases, first-principles reasoning can lead to more radical changes, creating transformative innovations.

# CHAPTER 3

# The Fallacy of the Next Big Thing

**Every company is continually looking for the next** big thing. I can't count the number of times I have heard executives say something along the lines of, "I want to know what's going to be the next iPhone before it becomes the next iPhone." Corporations are looking for someone to tell them what trends and products are going to be the big hits. Once they know what the next big thing is (ideally, before everyone else knows about it), they can invest early, create a dominant presence, and reap the rewards. Simple.

Unfortunately, it does not work that way. While my research on innovation has revealed some distinct factors necessary to create breakthrough offerings, it also highlighted some of the misconceptions and fallacies that impede corporations as they try to become more innovative. One of the prime misconceptions in the corporate world today is that companies must continually quest for the next big thing.

There are three problems with looking for the next big thing. They are, in order, (1) next, (2) big, and (3) thing.

Let's look at each of them.

## Next

Rarely do innovations and trends take the world by surprise. One of the consistent themes in the history of innovation is the concept of slow burn, or a slow evolution. Most industry trends are visible and provide clues about the next breakthrough. A few years ago, the Corporate Strategy team at a large technology company revisited a strategic plan it had developed over a decade ago. The purpose was to see how accurate its predictions of technology trends were, based on how many of its decade-plus predictions had come true. This was an interesting exercise. The strategy team had done a remarkably accurate job in predicting the major trends and developments that would shape the technology sector, with only a few misses. The innovations that occurred over that decade were not entirely a surprise; they had been predicted by the various sensing and insights teams across the company.

Most innovations in history have had a slow evolution process. Things move slowly, but not because they have to; rather, it is because people often don't see the value in what is being developed and don't adopt the innovations. The printing press took centuries to become a breakthrough innovation. The earliest use of paper currency, an innovation used in ancient China for trade, was known by the Western world centuries before it was adopted; however, the notion of using paper to represent value (instead of gold, something tangible and with obvious value) was a far-fetched concept. It took almost eighty years to get from the introduction of the first lightbulb to Thomas Edison's mass-market lightbulb. It took a decade after Alexander Fleming's discovery and publication of the wonder-drug penicillin for another group of scientists to take further action and develop it as a drug effective for treating people with infections.

The point is that the next breakthrough is often not a secret. It is already here. For most large companies, the next breakthrough is probably being developed within their own corporation. We just saw two examples—Kodak developing a digital camera, and Xerox developing a computer mouse—where neither company recognized the value of developments within their own walls, though they were likely looking outside their organization for the next thing. These companies are hardly alone. The hundreds of thousands of patents and new developments within corporations show that the problem is not that breakthrough ideas are not being generated; they are simply not being recognized, and their potential remains unrealized.

We have known this for a long time. The diffusion of innovation theory, one of the oldest social science theories, explains that the spread of an innovation follows an S curve. Innovations start off slowly, transition into a rapid high-growth state, and then slow down during the maturity phase. The slow initial phase gives us enough time to identify the evolving technologies in the pipeline and react to them. We just need to know which ones to react to, and we need to react faster.

A few years ago, a large consumer products company engaged one of the companies I managed for a strategic assignment: identify the next big waves of innovation in their market space. It challenged us to tell it something it didn't know: the next big thing. We did a thorough job identifying the innovations that would shape the consumer products space over the coming decade. We went through a sophisticated exercise to try and predict the future. We looked at what patents were being filed, what products were being created by startups, what research was being done by governments and universities, what industry experts were saying, where funding was going, and many other sources to develop a comprehensive list of potential disruptors and creations that could truly enhance lives around the world. The problem with this process was that our client was one of the largest corporations in the world, and one employee or another was familiar with at least one new trend and disruptor on our list. This information was not institutional knowledge within the corporation, because pockets of the company knew only some of the things, but the corporation as a whole had already been exposed—somewhere in its vast silos—to all the potential waves of innovation.

In the technology industry, where I spent the majority of my career, the trends have always been clear. They were the personal computer, the Internet, mobile devices, the smartphone, and the cloud. Today the trends include artificial intelligence, machine learning, and other developments. The innovators were the ones who rode these trends to create fantastic products that customers embraced. They created business models that produced gravity-defying profits, and ecosystems that built a generation of entry barriers. Microsoft did not create the first computer operating system. Google did not create the first search engine. Facebook did not create the first social platform. Apple did not create the first portable music player or the first smartphone. None of these trends were a secret; they were available to everyone to build societal value. None of these companies were first to market; instead they did it better or engaged their users in better ways.

While there will always be valuable new developments, the challenge for companies is to recognize the existing developments in the world and to make the right bets. They have to build value from what is out there now. This is what separates the true innovators from the ones who are just looking for the next thing to jump onto. True innovators build, create, and transform. They don't simply adopt a new development; they create something new and valuable with it.

## Big

The second fallacy of the continual search for the next big thing is "big." Looking at the history of innovations, rarely does something become big right from the start, and rarely does the innovator know that what they are developing is going to change the world. Few world-changing innovations started with a view to change the world. Few billion-dollar businesses started with a view to earn a billion dollars. The one thing they had in common was that they altered customer experience through a unique approach and, in the process, created an immense amount of value for their users.

Corporations, both large and small, are wired to think big. Part of the corporate DNA dictates that only if you make big and bold plans will you be able to shape the world. Almost all management gurus advise companies to think big, make big bets, and think about big, hairy, audacious goals. Yes, it is important to think big, but companies need to think big in terms of inspiring customers and transforming experiences, not think big solely in terms of P&L impact. Financial rewards automatically follow a big change in experience. Understandably, in order to make a P&L impact, large corporations require big bets that pay off. They need to generate hundreds of millions, or even perhaps a few billion dollars, in incremental revenue gains every year simply to maintain a modest growth rate; naturally, this creates a strong temptation to implement the plans and ideas that show the biggest impact to growth and profitability. However, it is hard to create a billion-dollar business without creating a smaller business first. And unfortunately, many promising small plans get pushed aside in favor of bigger business plans that look great on paper but require a vast investment to pull off—and often don't deliver on their promise.

Google, today's Internet heavyweight, started off as an academic experiment by two doctoral students as a way to understand how web pages are connected to each other and to develop a better index for the Web. The idea was that you could determine the importance or rank of a website by looking at how many other web pages are linked to it and how many other web pages are linked to each of them.

Initially this wasn't even a commercial initiative. Building the world's leading search engine, which led to Google being the Internet's most dominant player and one of the most valuable companies on the planet, was far from anyone's imagination. Relevant search results were simply a by-product of the index they had created. Soon, the founders noticed that their search results were markedly superior to other existing search engines of the time. In fact, shortly after Google's creation, its founders were ready to sell their company to Excite, one of the leading search engines of the time, for under a million dollars. Excite refused.

As we know now, Google became big—very big. The "big" happened not by executing a plan to build a world-changing company, but by providing a big improvement to the experience of users—a large *experience delta*, the difference between the current experience and the new one. The business model (based on advertising revenues) that created over half a trillion dollars of market value was not part of a grand plan, but as the company increased its value to society, society figured out a way to reward the company.

The printing press was developed to ease the process of printing. The massive success of the printing press was the longest of long shots. Had the idea been presented within today's corporate environment, or even to a venture capital fund, it might likely have been laughed out of the conference room. It certainly would not have been approved. Who would want to invest in a product that eased the process of printing books when most of the population could not even read? In today's vernacular, the total addressable market was virtually zero and would remain nonexistent for the foreseeable future (during the years it would take each user to become literate). Yet this invention spurred literacy worldwide and transferred power from the elite few to the broader population. It is certainly one of the greatest innovations of all time.

The impact of the printing press is only matched by the introduction of the Internet, another innovation that gave enormous power to the masses. It began, quite humbly, as a way to send information from one computer to another, primarily in academic and research settings, through a technique called *packet switching*— breaking data down into small chunks, or packets, before sending them to another computer.

The list goes on and on. Uber started with three cars to provide a better service than a taxi, not to become a verb for the *uberization* of every industry. The founders of Airbnb turned their own loft into a lodging space and advertised it, without a plan to create the largest home-share network. Or consider a less obvious innovation: Instant replay was an innovation that revolutionized how we watch sports on TV (and even how sports outcomes are determined). Instant replay was originally a small experiment by a young TV producer named Tony Verna. He simply wanted to try and improve the broadcast and fill in some dead time between plays of the Army–Navy game in 1963.

In looking for the next billion-dollar opportunity, corporations spend countless hours doing strategic planning and modeling how their new initiatives will generate massive financial returns. I may be stating the obvious here, but breakthroughs rarely come from strategic planning or elaborate financial forecasting. In many instances, corporations make large investments in the wrong areas because strategic-planning exercises lead them down the wrong path. Most strategic plans focus either on assumptions, which are fraught with risk, or on costs, a variable that is entirely under management's control. These plans rarely focus on customer experiences, because these are nebulous, or on products that inspire customers on a small scale, because although these small changes might add up to enormous changes for society as a whole, they don't visibly move the corporate needle.

Worse yet, inspiring ideas and innovations that could be breakthroughs often get shoved aside (like the first digital camera developed at Kodak) because they don't fit with the existing business model or have a billion-dollar plan. I have seen many potentially great ideas fail because they did not get the right attention or have a large enough contribution, or they got subsumed by a larger and more profitable business unit. Any of these factors can impede a small business from achieving its full potential and becoming bigger than you can imagine.

So keep in mind that the big opportunity you are chasing may actually appear as something quite small. The key is to learn to recognize the opportunities that alter experiences and to understand and articulate how these customer experiences are transformed. Once you can do this, even at a small scale, the chances are high you'll find the right opportunities that will evolve into the big game changers we are all looking for.

## Thing

The third flaw in the relentless search for the next big thing is the "thing." My research has shown that there are two main problems with this. The first is that an innovation is often not a physical thing—a product. The second misleading aspect of "thing" is that the value of the innovation is often not in the thing that is being developed; the real value is in how an invention is supported— something I call the "thing behind the thing." Let me explain both of these misconceptions.

## THE THING IS NOT A THING

First, while most companies are focusing on innovation through creating new products, many disruptions come instead from a change in business model. American Airlines revolutionized flying by popularizing the concept of frequent-flyer miles. It was still selling the same airline seats, but the innovation that transformed how we think about air travel was simply a program designed to reward those who fly more. The frequent-flyer program induced a sense of loyalty rarely seen in any product. Frequent-flyer miles, which included free travel and first-class upgrades, were a tangible, material, and highly coveted reward for simply flying on American Airlines instead of another airline. The costs to the company were miniscule, as it simply used unsold seats as rewards for its best customers. It was the perfect win-win for the customer and the company, resulting in what can be considered one of the greatest loyalty programs of all time.

Amazon Prime has played a substantial role in the rapid growth in revenues and valuation of Amazon.com, but it is not a product. Prime was initially a membership program where customers paid seventy-nine dollars a year and got free two-day shipping on virtually anything they purchased at Amazon.com, a novel concept at the time that customers found incredibly valuable. Prior to the introduction of Prime, express shipping on online purchases was not a common occurrence and was typically used only for special occasions. The time required for items to arrive through regular shipping dissuaded many shoppers from buying online. Enter Prime from Amazon.com, a membership program that not only reduced the time for a product to arrive but also guaranteed a delivery date. Customers loved it and the company loved it. Amazon Prime became one of the most successful online-shopping programs, ultimately altering the shape of Internet commerce. It is another example of the perfect win-win for both a company and its customers. Today, if Amazon Prime were a country, it would be roughly the twentieth-largest country in the world.

The ubiquitous Microsoft Office, one of the most successful franchises in the history of business, has generated hundreds of billions of dollars in revenue since its inception. Microsoft Office wasn't a thing; it was simply a change from selling three productivity applications (Word, Excel, and PowerPoint) as separate programs to selling them as a bundle. This created immense value for customers, who could buy an entire suite of applications for a single low price, and the company, which benefited from being the virtually sole provider of these applications. Once again, it is the perfect win-win for the customer and the company.

As illustrated in the examples above, companies have always enjoyed unparalleled success not by selling things but by providing value in other ways. This trend continues. Recently, companies like Uber and Airbnb have built tens or hundreds of billions of dollars of value not through product development in the traditional sense, but by connecting customers to rides and lodging. Innovation can come in many forms, and even if you are a product company, it would be wise not to think about innovation as solely the creation of new products.

## THE THING BEHIND THE THING

The second issue with focusing on the "thing" is that the invention we think of as being the innovation is often not the main creation—it is something else. Sometimes, the key to the success of an innovation is an entire system of supporting developments. These supporting developments are the thing behind the thing, essential elements without which there wouldn't be an innovation. For example, everybody thinks of the wheel as one of the greatest inventions of all time, enabling the first information and commerce highway in history. When you study the invention of the wheel, you learn that creating the wheel was the easy part; the hard part was connecting it to a stable platform. The true innovation was in the development of the axle, and it was the combination of the wheel and the axle that allowed the wheel to have a transformative effect on society. The axle was the thing behind the thing.

While Alexander Fleming is credited for the discovery of penicillin (the thing), it was virtually impossible to get pure penicillin in large enough quantities to treat even one person. The genius— the thing behind the thing—was in figuring out how to create substantial amounts of pure penicillin and thereby save millions of lives. The telegraph, created by Samuel Morse and his team and considered one of the greatest inventions of all time, was not valuable without the code to simplify the transmission of complex messages (Morse code). These are just a few examples of the thing behind the thing.

More recently, in the 1970s and 1980s many companies raced to be the dominant force in making and selling personal computers. Everyone focused on building computers, since that was the innovation. And, yes, the invention of the personal computer (PC) will always go down as one of the greatest innovations in history, but the thing that made it valuable and indispensable was the software that ran it and let you do magic with it. Today we know that far greater value has been created by the software (the thing behind the thing) than by the thing itself (the PC).

## How to think about innovation in light of the next-big-thing fallacy

This chapter is not intended to dissuade you from trying to build the next big thing. There will always be a next big thing, even if it's not technically next, big, or even a thing. There will be another iPhone, a new mode of transportation, or a blockbuster drug that cures cancer. These are all worthy pursuits. The reason I discuss the fallacy of the next big thing is that the language we use often guides how we think. If you only talk about the next big thing, you're going to be looking outward, somewhere else, for something new and big. In fact, the real innovation may already be right in front of you, not large, and in a form you can't yet define. If you limit your thinking, you may simply fail to recognize it.

Typically, companies looking for the next big thing are usually the ones whose growth has slowed or stalled. And when growth has slowed, looking outward for the next big thing distracts from the activity they should be primarily focusing on. They should be looking inward, reflecting on what got them to where they are in the first place.

Given the fallacies about the next big thing, your company should take a new approach when thinking about innovation. To start with, you need to have a deep-seated understanding of the trends in your business and of new developments that are being worked on within your own organization, other companies in your sector, and other sectors. We have learned from the history of innovations that the next idea is already here. The pieces are visible for everyone to see, and the one who puts them together in a compelling fashion is going to drive the wave of innovation. The answer, however, is not going to be obvious. You will need to put the right approaches in place to understand how you can meaningfully augment your customer's experience. (One hint: Don't ask your customers. They don't know.)

You will also need to experiment more and increase the number of new bets you make. Your rate of success will increase once you have a culture of innovation—when launching new offerings to customers is part of your company's DNA. Not all the new bets will have breakthrough success, but if you get in the habit of launching offerings geared toward transforming customer experiences, the rate of innovation will increase.

Finally, don't think about new product introduction as the only way to innovate. Think about all the other forces that can make your product more successful. Think of the things behind the thing. Think of ancillary benefits that can provide insanely high customer value and make an existing product irresistible. If your corporation adopts this mindset, you increase your likelihood of creating groundbreaking innovations that inspire and enhance your customers' lives.

# CHAPTER 4

# The Biome—The Greatest Innovator in the Universe

**We are living in an age where the** only real advantage a corporation has for sustained success is innovation. Large corporations that are powerful in many industries, have strong brands that are household names, and seem to be indispensable, can become irrelevant overnight.

Think about Borders: At one time, it was one of the most successful bookstores in the world. Borders' revenues in 2001 exceeded $3 billion, and it employed over thirty thousand people. In 2011, after years of declining revenues, Borders filed for bankruptcy.

BlackBerry was the proud maker of the businessperson's must-have communication device in 2011, with peak revenues of almost $20 billion. Today, just six short years later, it is a small shell of what it was, with revenues just a little over a billion dollars. It's a company trying to reinvent itself, without much success. What could possibly have gone wrong with such a darling of Wall Street?

Blockbuster was the undisputed heavyweight of video rentals, with eight thousand stores across the country in 2004. Just six years later, after several failed attempts at growth (organic and through acquisitions), the company was delisted from the New York Stock Exchange. Soon thereafter, it filed for bankruptcy. One misstep along the way was refusing to act when a little company named Netflix approached it for an investment and partnership opportunity.

The list of out-of-favor companies goes on and on: Polaroid, Nokia, Kodak, Motorola, Sears, and so many more. These companies, once a venerable who's who of corporate strength, are now dead or dying. And you never know who is going to be next. Disruptive competition can come from anywhere and at any time, and it is not just technology companies that are creating disruption through the implementation of digital solutions. A decade ago, who would have thought Levi's would face competition from yoga wear?

Almost any company can be turned upside down in virtually no time. It took Apple just a shade over two years to go from the start of iPhone development to the working model shown to the world.[14] And this was a complex development and production effort. All the pieces that Apple used to create the first iPhone were available to everyone. The innovation was in putting it all together

---

14  Fred Vogelstein, "And Then Steve Said, 'Let There Be an iPhone,'" *New York Times* (October 4, 2013), http://nytimes.com/2013/10/06/magazine/and-then-steve-said-let-there-be-an-iphone.html.

in a beautiful package, creating tremendous value coupled with ease of use, and establishing it as a must-have status symbol.

In most cases, everything required to make an experience-altering innovation possible is already available. Whether it is technology, know-how, or components, the necessary building blocks are likely available and reasonably easy to access right now. In almost every case, the innovators are the people or organizations who connect the dots to create new value from existing elements.

Today, anyone with financing, a dream or a vision, and courage can develop the next breakthrough and make it a reality. Dreams have never been in short supply, and financing from venture funds is abundant and ready to help transform those dreams into lasting, game-changing businesses. Those same dreams (and a larger source of funds) are prevalent within large corporations, and they can be realized through the development of an innovation biome.

## The right habitat for innovation

My model of innovation is based on the system that has, throughout time, been the single most successful environment for breakthrough creation. I am talking about the natural environment that supports life. The natural world around us is the most remarkable system, offering the conditions for certain biological innovations and creations to thrive while others perish.

The largest and most significant natural environments on the planet are called *biomes*. A biome is a large region of the earth that nurtures a certain set of plant and animal life. Biomes include vast areas and environments like the tundra, deciduous and tropical forests, grasslands, and deserts. A biome is not an ecosystem, although it may contain several biological ecosystems, which are groups of interconnected elements forming an interactive community.

The environments provided by biomes are critical to the creation and maintenance of a thriving and naturally innovative community. Biomes change over time, and human actions can affect them positively or negatively, impacting their productivity and output.

Think of your company as a biome, with its own resident ecosystems that include networked elements such as departments, teams, approaches, structures, rules, and other interconnections that continually interact with each other and, hopefully, flourish.

For example, there is a marketing ecosystem, with its own set of players and interconnections among advertising, account executives, data, and customers. There is a sales ecosystem, with its own set of interconnections among the sales team, their clients, the product or service, and other departments in the company. There is a product development ecosystem, connecting manufacturing with R&D and product design. These ecosystems are designed to work together, to collaborate and grow together, but they may also clash. In any case, they all live within the same environment (the biome, your company) and thrive or fail as one. More than anything else, your corporate biome determines how successful your company is in developing a sustained culture of innovation.

The natural biome is an ever-evolving environment whose fundamental characteristics determine how much growth and creation there will be within it. Characteristics like temperature, moisture, season, and soil are some of the most basic factors that affect the productivity of a biome. And each of these attributes determines whether a biome will be successful in creating breakthroughs.

Take seasons as an example. The longer the growing season, the more productive a biome is in developing and sustaining new life. Using our analogy, innovation also requires a long growing season. It needs time to germinate, take root under the surface, then finally sprout and grow. Unfortunately, in many companies, innovation efforts are characterized by one-off initiatives such as periodic innovation contests. There is nothing wrong with an innovation contest or with any specific initiative in and of itself, but the fact that these initiatives are intermittent—rather than woven into the fabric of the company—means that the innovation biome is almost guaranteed to be fruitless. And this is simply because the growing season for innovation is a series of short bursts.

Your corporate biome can be a cold tundra, characterized by a permanently frozen layer of soil that prevents the growth of new trees. Or it can be a tropical rainforest, with large and dense growth, abundant life, and high levels of productivity.

Innovation activities are like the soil in the rainforest. It is not the most fertile, but it is likely to nurture the trees that are already growing. Growing multiple trees creates the highest probability that one of them will break through the canopy. In the rainforest, the majestic kapok tree is one such breakthrough, growing to over 200 feet and towering over everything else in the rainforest. With a trunk that can grow up to 10 feet in diameter, it is truly a giant, dominating everything within its landscape.

Metaphorically, every corporation is in a continual search for its own kapok tree and looking for the great ideas that can get it there. It has to, simply because of the law of large numbers. The smallest company in the Fortune 1000 list has annual revenues of almost $2 billion. Each of these companies needs a minimum annual growth of hundreds of millions, if not billions, of dollars just to have a growth rate that is acceptable to its shareholders and other stakeholders like customers and employees. In addition, it needs to protect its multibillion-dollar franchise from being eaten up by established or upstart competitors. It is no wonder that every corporation is searching for its own kapok tree.

However, if the history of innovations has taught us anything, it is that the search for the big breakthrough is unlikely to result in one. I am reminded of the old fable of the young cat chasing itself in circles because it believed that happiness lay within its tail. As hard as the cat tried to catch its tail, the tail kept eluding it. An older and wiser cat watched the first cat spin furiously for a while and then said, "You'll never catch it. But why are you chasing it anyway? If you simply go about your business, it will follow you wherever you go." The same is true of innovation: If you stop chasing it and simply make it a part of yourself, a part of your organization, it will always be there. The innovation biome helps you stop chasing your tail.

The role of the corporation is to act as a fertile biome and provide the environment that enables innovations, which in turn make the big breakthroughs possible. And just like within a natural biome, many small things have to happen, and they need to happen every day and all the time to create the big breakthrough. The big breakthroughs are possible, even with imperfect ideas, just as the nutrient-deprived soil of the rainforest nurtures huge trees.

But you need a system for planting multiple seeds—a system for putting all reasonable ideas to work and ensuring that the elements and conditions supporting innovation are present.

Biodiversity within ecosystems and biomes, the interactions between diverse forms of life, is a hallmark of productivity that leads to new growth. Your corporation requires a similar environment for ideas to clash, combine, and collaborate in order to create an innovation biome.

## Natural selection of innovation

The development and adoption of innovations generally follow well-established laws of nature. In 1859, Charles Darwin introduced his theory of natural selection. The core concept of this theory is that traits that were useful to life were preserved, whereas others were not. The individuals best adapted to their environment were most likely to survive. Furthermore, Darwin believed that evolutionary change is gradual and slow, and because population growth for every species is rapid, there is constant competition for resources.

The theory of natural selection teaches us that there is a constant struggle and competition among species for natural resources. Any trait developed by an organism must be heritable (be transmittable to offspring) and offer a relative advantage over the competition in order to persist.

Innovation is much the same. Ideas or developments of value—those with a competitive advantage—survive the test of time. They morph and grow, and they are passed on through generations. The best ideas rarely resemble their original avatar. They have evolved, sometimes unrecognizably, and manifested themselves in many of the great discoveries of all time. Great developments have crossed industries, been refined, and sometimes been lost for years, decades, or centuries. But the best ideas have always survived and revealed themselves in ways that are unexpected, causing an indescribable impact to society.

Through the development of a productive biome, innovation can be institutionalized and become a core competency within your organization—it can be woven into the fabric of the business. Innovation is not just a buzzword. You can't claim to be innovative while showing marginal growth year after year. Simply investing heavily in R&D isn't enough. You must make innovation an integral part of your company to create offerings that are truly loved by your customers. To develop the innovation biome, you need to adopt a framework that is clear and well understood across the organization, a framework that is replicable and measurable and has the full support of the organization. This is the only way to make innovation a function that delivers value that your company and all its employees can be proud of.

## Integrating innovation

Companies have specialized in brand management, with specific objectives, activities, and metrics. Companies have specialized in strategic planning, operational management and efficiency, talent-development programs, financial planning, and customer support. Companies have also specialized in R&D programs that push the boundaries of science. Yet innovation, the activity most likely to provide sustained and long-term value and customer excitement, remains a vague function with no real accountability and no fixed methodology or set of tools. In fact, even within the same company, departments often treat innovation differently, with diverse metrics and approaches.

Corporations today have implemented a wide range of activities designed to spur innovation, including the following:

- Creating innovation departments
- Implementing innovation platforms
- Increasing R&D investment
- Acquiring innovative companies
- Creating internal startups
- Creating external startups
- Developing a better understanding of unmet customer needs
- Creating skunkworks projects
- Using lean techniques
- Establishing venture investments teams
- Establishing innovation competitions
- Using old-fashioned idea boxes

Sometimes companies may provide employees with time off to work on pet projects, be innovative, and pursue new ideas. They incentivize new product creation, and they try not to penalize failure. They often outsource their innovation efforts to consultants tasked with finding new opportunities and generating promising ideas, but each consultant has their own methodology that may conflict with another approach. Or sometimes organizations think of innovation as the result of design and creativity and have sessions intended to spur executive creativity.

Each of these approaches has its merits. However, if a single approach to innovation worked consistently and resulted in corporations accelerating the rate of innovation, then we would all be using it. There are best practices in marketing, sales, finance, strategy, operations management, and other functions, but not in innovation. The only way forward is to follow a structure and a set of principles that make innovation an everyday, integral part of your organization. An innovation biome lets you systemically drive the creation of breathtaking and inspirational new offerings by making innovation intrinsic to your identity and existence.

# PART 2

---

# THE ATTRIBUTES
# OF INNOVATION

**Innovations come in all flavors. Sometimes they happen** fortuitously or serendipitously. An invention can happen suddenly when the inventor stumbles upon something novel and unusual, often while doing something else, and societal acceptance of the new creation takes everyone—especially the inventor—by surprise.

Sildenafil, a drug developed to treat high blood pressure and angina, had an unusual side effect that was observed during clinical trials. This led to the creation of a newly advertised problem (erectile dysfunction) along with the solution to it: Viagra, a drug that has racked up tens of billions of dollars in revenue.

Or take potato chips as an example. As is widely reported, they were created by George Crum, a cook in upstate New York. As the story goes, a customer repeatedly sent his french fries back because they were not done right. After a couple of attempts to make them just right, an exasperated Crum decided he had had enough, and in an attempt to infuriate the diner, he developed a concoction he thought would taste terrible. He sliced the potatoes thinly, fried them until they were extra crisp, and added way too much salt. To Crum's surprise, the customer—and, soon, everybody else—loved them.

Sometimes innovations are created to solve an observed need or even one's own needs; necessity can indeed be the mother of invention. In 1902, Mary Anderson, an Alabama native visiting New York City, saw the driver of her trolley struggle with keeping the windshield clean during a storm. The driver had to either fold the glass down or stop and get out of the trolley to clear the windshield. Off went the proverbial lightbulb in her head, and a year later she came up with a solution: a swinging arm with a rubber blade to wipe moisture off the windshield. Sadly, as is true in so many cases, she tried shopping the idea to companies to manufacture, but no one was interested. Sure enough, the windshield wiper is now one innovation we cannot live without.

Over a century later, San Francisco was the setting for a similar story of necessity generating an invention. A couple of roommates, feeling the pain of the high rent for their loft, decided to sublet their living room, offering air mattresses and a homemade breakfast. Three visitors at a nearby convention took them up on their offer, and Airbnb (initially known as airbedandbreakfast) was born.

Sometimes, transformational innovations are the result of a larger vision or the work involved in making that vision a reality. In 1907, Henry Ford articulated a vision to "create a car for the multitude." This was at a time when every automobile was custom built and accessible only to the wealthy. He figured the only way he could deliver on his vision was to significantly bring down the cost of making a car. While this endeavor has resulted in many innovations, such as mass-manufactured, standardized and interchangeable parts, his greatest innovation, the one that fully enabled him to realize his vision, was the creation of the assembly line. This was a novel concept that completely flipped the model of building cars. With the creation of the assembly line, the work came to the worker and not the other way around. Partially finished automobiles moved from station to station, where different parts and components were sequentially added, leading to a finished product at the end of the line. The workers did not have to be skilled artisans; they simply had to be trained for a single task, which created a large and available pool of labor and resulted in an even greater production of cars. The time it took to assemble a car dropped from twelve hours to under two hours, and the cost of building a vehicle came down from $850 to $260[15] ($3,500 in today's dollars). The efficiency of the assembly line was largely responsible for increasing manufacturing productivity from one hundred cars a day to one thousand cars a day—a tenfold improvement.

Innovation in the private sector is often an outcome of government-funded research. NASA alone is responsible for countless innovations we take for granted today, including the following:

- Portable cordless vacuums
- Memory foam mattresses
- Enriched baby food
- LEDs

---

15  AFP/Relaxnews, "Ford's Assembly Line Turns 100: How It Changed Manufacturing and Society," *New York Daily News* (October 7, 2013).

- Artificial limbs
- Infrared ear thermometers
- Robotic surgery

This last one—minimally invasive surgery aided by robotics—has revolutionized surgery. Incisions are smaller, the risk of infection is much lower, and recovery is quicker. This innovation was developed through a desire for (and funding from) the US Army to allow a surgeon to operate on a wounded soldier remotely.

Government-funded research also resulted in the Internet, walkie-talkies, GPS systems, and many other technologies and products we rely on every day.

Significant breakthroughs that have remarkably changed how we live and operate share some themes that you can follow in your organization. As you might imagine, each innovation story is unique, and there are countless factors that contribute to the development of each great innovation. Fortunately, most innovations cluster around a set of distinct attributes or themes. The five broad attributes of innovation in the following list have been true for centuries, are true today, and will be true centuries from now.

1. Priming

2. Acceptance

3. Networked development

4. Clusters of value

5. A catalytic environment

Understanding and applying these five themes can help companies develop an innovation biome. Establishing the presence of these attributes within your company will increase your chances of creating an environment where innovation can thrive and become an integral part of your organization. This will lead to a culture where big breakthroughs are expected, not simply desired.

We'll look at each attribute one at a time in the subsequent chapters.

# CHAPTER 5

# Priming Innovation

**Self-taught tinkerer and engineer Percy Spencer became an** expert in radar tube design. He worked for Raytheon, a large defense contractor for the US. During World War II, Spencer was responsible for working on magnetrons, vacuum tubes used to build radar equipment.

One day in the lab, he reached into his pocket for a candy bar and found it had melted. A different researcher might have looked at his melted candy bar and cursed the heavens for petty irritations while licking chocolate from his fingers. He might have adjusted the air conditioning or put the candy aside and forgotten about it. But Spencer was deeply familiar with the radiation emitted by his magnetrons, and he immediately wondered whether that could be the cause of his softened confection. After some experimentation, he discovered that the microwaves generated by the magnetron induced the molecules in food to produce thermal energy, heating the food quickly and efficiently. Quite accidentally—and only because he had expert knowledge of the subject—Spencer had invented the microwave oven.

Although this was not the first observation of microwaves in action, it was Spencer's prepared, or *primed*, mind that led him to believe he had hit on something and to investigate what the melted candy bar meant. Today, the microwave oven is a staple in over 90 percent of American households. Incidentally, popcorn was one of the first things Spencer used to test the microwave.

As the Percy Spencer example shows, inadvertent innovations happen only when the mind is prepared to recognize something as exceptional. That can happen either when you have deep foundational knowledge of a subject or when you think about a problem long and hard for an extended period of time. One day, when you least expect it, the solution seemingly serendipitously comes to you.

The archetypal story about a primed mind making a discovery is the oft-retold story of Archimedes, one of the greatest Greek mathematicians and engineers. His ruler asked him to solve a problem: How could they authenticate the amount of gold in his crown? When Archimedes settled into a bathtub one day and noticed the water in the tub overflow, the solution popped into his mind. He realized he could determine the volume of an object based on the volume of water it displaces. This became the now-famous Archimedes principle, or the law of buoyancy. As the story goes, he jumped out of his bathtub and ran into the streets of Syracuse—naked—shouting, "Eureka! Eureka!" ("I found it!").

Eureka moments are flashes of insight. Suddenly, pieces of a puzzle create the perfect shape, and everything makes sense. These eureka moments have their stamp on many of the greatest discoveries in the world—in science, in medicine, and in every other field. Many of these moments came while someone was doing something unrelated, even sleeping and dreaming.

August Kekulé, one of the pioneers of organic chemistry, discerned the ring structure of the benzene molecule, one of the most important compounds in organic chemistry, from a dream where he saw a serpent biting its own tail. Organic chemistry owes an eternal debt to this dream. To be clear, the dream came after Kekulé's intense study of the subject, after he had developed advanced knowledge of the nature of carbon bonds. With his deep knowledge of the topic, Kekulé required only the right inspiration to be able to connect all the pieces.

Thomas Edison, one of the world's most prolific inventors, understood this and worked hard at preparing, or priming, his mind for innovative undertakings. In his own words, "When I want to discover something, I begin by reading up everything that has been done along that line in the past. That's what all these books in the library are there for."[16] Thorough absorption of the available knowledge is how you prepare for innovation.

In 1928, Alexander Fleming made one of the most profound observations in the history of medicine. After he returned from vacation, he sorted through petri dishes containing *Staphylococcus*

---

16  Wikipedia, "Edisonian approach" (2017), https://en.wikipedia.org/wiki/Edisonian_approach.

(a bacterium that causes sore throats, among other things). All of his petri dishes contained colonies of the bacteria—except for one dish, which had some mold growing on it. The area around the mold was clear. His knowledge of the experiment and bacteria primed him to realize that the mold was killing the bacteria. He eventually discovered that it hindered a wide range of harmful bacteria. This observation, made possible only by a mind that was primed and prepared, led to the discovery of antibiotics, which have since saved hundreds of millions of lives.

These innovators, from Archimedes to Fleming, were deeply consumed by their efforts to develop solutions for vexing problems, and their primed minds recognized the significance of unrelated events—whether it was an overflowing bathtub, a dream, or a moldy dish. They saw the possibilities because they were prepared.

If you think about a problem hard enough, it persists in the back of your mind no matter what you are doing. You may not even notice it, but this constant percolation, in which the problem is an integral part of your—or your company's—thinking, can lead to ideas that simply couldn't be imagined in an innovation contest or focus group. After enough percolation, finally something most unexpected clicks, and you have your eureka moment.

We've all experienced this feeling at some point, but it doesn't have to be purely accidental. It can be fostered, and it can be replicated. You can't predict when your eureka moment will hit, but you can create an environment perfect for that moment to occur.

The message for us is simple: Innovation is not going to happen if your mind is not ready to understand the transformative power of what is happening right in front of you. Groundbreaking opportunities are passed up repeatedly, until the right opportunity meets the primed mind. As Hungarian Nobel laureate Albert Szent-Györgyi eloquently said, "A discovery is said to be an accident meeting a prepared mind."[17]

The corporate mind can be primed just like the individual's. Large corporations that have the brightest people, who spend vast amounts of money on interesting original research, and build on their science as well as the science of others, have their share of breakthroughs.

However, corporations often fail to capitalize on these creations, and many potentially brilliant inventions never make it to the marketplace. There are many organizational barriers that prevent the refinement, development, and productization of great ideas and promising observations and advances. Sometimes they are stuck in corporate bureaucracy, and the inventors are unable to make a stronger push for their ideas. Sometimes great ideas may not initially have a clear business benefit, and in the risk-averse corporate culture, no one wants to invest in ideas that don't immediately show a profit. Often, good ideas fail to get the attention or approval of senior managers and simply perish. Sometimes a new development may miss a product shipment cycle, or the management team may have different priorities, leaving a good idea hanging interminably. Sometimes inventions are viewed as just too farfetched for the company to contemplate, or they may seem counterintuitive to the current business model.

---

17  Philosophical Library, "Nobel Prize winner Albert Szent-Györgyi is 123 Today!" (2017), http://www.philosophicallibrary.com/nobel-prize-winner-albert-szent-gyorgyi-is-123-today/.

For your company to thrive on innovation, it must excel at identifying ideas and game-changing opportunities that are sitting right in front of it. In many companies, there is often little knowledge of the potential developments in product or R&D departments. A good first step for priming your corporate mind is to map out the idea-to-development flow and understand why new product development or R&D investments are not creating products that get used by customers. The development of an innovation map is critical to getting a corporation primed for innovation. First and foremost, such a map illustrates whether the organization is even ready to innovate. You can build this innovation-readiness map by following the journey of innovation from the time an idea or development is introduced to the moment when it goes into development and reaches customers or is abandoned somewhere along the way. This exercise is certain to highlight the barriers preventing ideas from germinating and becoming value-enhancing offerings.

Your company also needs a simple and replicable methodology to evaluate how new developments can impact society. Don't just make initial judgments solely on near-term P&L impact. Evaluate how much of an improvement an innovation offers in altering an experience journey, the journey a potential customer takes to go through a task. The bigger the impact, or the larger the experience delta, the more likely the new development is going to be a success. This approach is discussed in detail in chapter 11.

Most corporate managers have been to off-site brainstorming meetings to develop new ideas for the organization, but as we all have experienced, such meetings usually fail to produce the hoped-for insights. The lack of a primed mind is the reason these corporate off-sites, which are designed to spur creativity, are usually unproductive. Creativity and grand new ideas do not appear on the days we clear our calendars to think about the corporate rainbow of white spaces and blue oceans and green dollar bills. It just does not work that way.

Building a primed organization provides the right environment to develop an innovation biome, which helps your own creations blossom and provide immense value to customers and society. Without it, great ideas, even those right in front of you, will go unnoticed.

CHAPTER 6

# Accepting Innovation

**An important observation in the history of medicine** was made
by Hungarian physician Ignaz Semmelweis in the mid-1800s.
Semmelweis noticed a remarkable difference between maternity
wards where physicians delivered babies and maternity wards
where midwives delivered babies. Mothers under the care of physicians had a five times greater chance of death from childbed fever
than those cared for by midwives.

After numerous experiments and observations, Semmelweis
hypothesized that the high death rate arose because physicians
were also scientists who dissected cadavers, whereas the midwives
did not. For some unexplained reasons, the physicians who delivered babies after working on cadavers unwittingly caused more
mothers to die.

Semmelweis tried many experiments to understand why, but the only one that reduced these untimely deaths was when he ordered his staff to start cleaning their hands and instruments with chlorine before delivering babies. In doing so, he stumbled on one of the most common actions we take for granted today: washing hands to prevent disease.

Semmelweis showed that physicians could save countless lives with a simple activity like washing their hands, although he could not explain the reasons why his method was effective (because Louis Pasteur's theory of germs had not yet been introduced to the world). Regardless, with so many lives that could potentially be saved, Semmelweis should have been a hero with his discovery. Instead, the medical community rejected his findings and laughed him off as a lunatic. Doctors were outraged by the notion that their unwashed hands caused their patients to die. They were, after all, noble gentlemen responsible for saving lives. The fact that they could be responsible in any way for unwittingly killing people was simply against their belief system, regardless of the empirical evidence to the contrary.

Conventional wisdom never results in innovation. There is always reluctance or even outright rejection of new ideas. Things that are patently obvious today were previously innovations rejected by conventional thinkers. Naysayers, disbelievers, and skeptics abound and have been a drag on innovation throughout history. Darwin was laughed at for his theory of evolution. The earth is round, you say? No way. The telephone will never be successful (presumably because there was no shortage of messenger boys), and Louis Pasteur's theory of germs is "ridiculous fiction."

According to experts, online shopping was never supposed to catch on, and neither was the iPhone, the PC, the TV, or the automobile.

Worse yet, the disbelief persists for a long time. Take Gregor Mendel, for example, the pioneer of genetics. Mendel taught the world about heredity and the passing of traits from one generation to another, but he died before his work was accepted by the scientific community.

## Internal reluctance

The opening chapter of this book covered the story of how the first digital camera was developed at Kodak in 1975 but was never brought to market. At that time, the camera was clunky and slow, and Kodak's management thought no one would want to view pictures on computers (which were also clunky and slow).

But there is more to the story. Fast forward to 1989. The same engineer, Steven Sasson (still at Kodak), and his colleague Robert Hills created the first modern digital single-lens reflex (DSLR) camera that looked and functioned like the ones available today. Now there were no excuses. The camera worked and was clearly a breakthrough.[18] This was Kodak's unlikely second chance at establishing the vision for photography for decades to come. However, their then-current value judgment, yet again, prevented them from bringing a digital product to market. This time, the marketing department wasn't interested, because the DSLR camera would hurt the company's film sales.

---

18  James Estrin, "Kodak's First Digital Moments," *New York Times* (August 12, 2015), https://lens.blogs.nytimes.com/2015/08/12/kodaks-first-digital-moment.

Every time we apply today's thinking to tomorrow's idea, we dilute its potential. In many companies, the people with the power to approve, impede, or reject an innovation are not the innovators. They may not see the possibilities of the innovation and don't have the primed mind so crucial for success.

There are occasional cases where innovations succeed in companies despite leaders who don't share the vision of an innovator. A story similar to the Kodak one, but with remarkably different results, is the Nespresso project at Nestlé, (a multinational consumer-products company successfully selling Nescafé, a leading brand for home coffee consumption). Building and selling expensive machines and even more expensive pods for single servings of coffee was not in the plans. The Nespresso project was the brainchild of Nestlé employee Eric Favre. It was halted soon after the project began, because his bosses feared it would dent Nescafé sales. However, Favre kept working on it in secret and eventually persuaded the company to let him try it with consumers. Nespresso became the most significant innovation in home coffee consumption since the paper filter and led to billions of dollars in revenue.

Nespresso is an example of a persistent employee overcoming disbelievers and secretly toiling away on a project he believed in, eventually creating a groundbreaking innovation. But this is not the norm. In most cases, projects that get quashed by managers stay quashed and never make it into production. With the right support, however, game-changing innovations are more likely to be developed and introduced to the world.

If you are not going to be the innovator, it is important not to be the naysayer. That simply depresses the rate of innovation.

Just because you don't see the possibilities of a new development does not mean the possibilities are not there. I have been guilty of not seeing the promise of new developments and have shelved and delayed projects because I could not see the potential at the time. Most business leaders are guilty of this, and it is a hard mindset to change, because you are investing real dollars and resources into ideas that you may not believe in and that have no certainty of success. As an innovation leader, you are responsible for placing the right bets (and some projects should be shelved). But by creating an organization-wide culture of innovation, you can multiply the number of ideas and enhance the possibilities for success.

## Conventional techniques

Conventional wisdom is not the only thing that prevents forward progress. Conventional research techniques often prevent great ideas from becoming breakthrough innovations. When ideas and projects worth pursuing are generated, companies usually engage in two activities to refine them and make them market ready, stating the following:

- "Let's test it out with customers and get their feedback."
- "Let's build a financial model so we know exactly what we are getting into."

The first activity is to get real-world reactions from customers, and the second is intended to predict revenues and profitability for the next few years, an exercise that will drive the go/no-go decision.

While both approaches often provide value, they are not good for developing and understanding innovations that are nonlinear, and they frequently prevent a great idea from achieving its potential. Unless the idea is so obvious and flawless that everyone who sees it for the first time will simply fall in love with it, traditional customer research and financial modeling are not going to be good indicators of its eventual success.

## MARKET RESEARCH

Breakthrough innovations, by their very definition, are novel offerings where the customer is undefined, so research is often directed to the wrong customer set. Often, the innovation concept is so new that research subjects are unable to provide meaningful feedback. As the Internet was evolving in the 1990s, I probably managed more research studying its impact than any other individual or organization. The one thing I learned was that consumers could never articulate the value that the Internet could offer. Had customer research and consumers, rather than the innovators, led the development of the Internet, we would not have made anywhere near the progress we have. Imagine doing market research on the printing press, which was developed at a time when the overwhelming majority of the population could not even read. Who were the customers? Likewise, no amount of market research would have predicted the success of the automobile or PC. There just weren't any markets to research.

Customer research is good for understanding usage, satisfaction, and perceptions; evaluating linear advances; prioritizing features; and making trade-offs between alternatives. However, if the innovation is unrelated or completely independent from what is currently available, there is no guarantee that customer research is going to point you in a marginally relevant direction—much less the right direction. The history of business is littered with innovations where market research has delivered false negatives, such as the development of ATMs ("Who in their right mind would trust a machine to handle their money?"), and false positives, such as the launch of New Coke (which did well in blind taste tests, but the research did not uncover that people had a stronger emotional connection to the traditional Coke brand than to the new drink).

Scott Anthony, in a 2008 article in the *Harvard Business Review*,[19] summarized the four biggest flaws with traditional market research approaches in innovation:

1. Talking to the wrong customers

2. Asking the wrong questions

3. Having the wrong people interpret the data

4. Making the wrong decisions based on the market research data

Techniques such as ethnography and observational research can help in the development of breakthrough innovations. However, these techniques are often underutilized or incorrectly applied.

---

19 Scott Anthony, "Four Ways Traditional Market Research Can Kill Innovation," *Harvard Business Review* (June 3, 2008), https://hbr.org/2008/06/four-ways -traditional-market-r.

Ethnography is an incredibly valuable tool for understanding consumer experiences. But it can only work if it is applied in the correct manner and if the experiences are viewed, unedited, by the right people.

## FINANCIAL MODELING

In addition to market research, the other conventional technique preventing the development of breakthroughs is financial modeling. Corporations routinely build a long-range financial model for every initiative they invest in. These models, often referred to as *discounted cash flow* (DCF) models, are valuable in many instances, but for predicting the returns from a breakthrough innovation, they are futile.

First, there is simply no concrete knowledge of the size of the market. Second, there is really no insight into how a breakthrough is going to be accepted and used, or the rate of adoption over time. A DCF model simply becomes a compounding of assumptions, which leads to chaos.

Now, because these models are built with stepwise logic and show a seemingly reasonable picture of how the investment into a new initiative will play out, they become believable and are assumed to be accurate. And we must be careful of that. For the same reasons that market research is risky, building DCF models for evaluating the risks and returns of breakthrough innovations leads to either grossly false negatives or grossly false positives. And they usually lead to the wrong decision.

# Nonlinear innovation

Nonlinear innovations are those that are not an obvious or direct improvement over a current offering. A linear innovation would suggest that a car offering 30 miles per gallon is better than one offering 20 miles per gallon, or a car with six cylinders is better than a car with four, and so on. Nonlinear innovations bring new value. Instead of going from 25 to 30 or even 50 miles per gallon, a nonlinear innovation would be one where no fuel is used, making the miles per gallon consideration irrelevant.

Launching an innovation is a risk that a company knowingly takes. Breakthroughs are about a tenfold improvement, or making something 10 times better than the current alternative. They are never about marginal improvement or making a product 10 percent better. Breakthroughs are about changing the game entirely through nonlinear developments, and because they are altogether new offerings, their market performance is unlikely to be modeled or researched accurately.

There is a real and material chance an innovation will not succeed. However, if the breakthrough you are developing is backed by your strong belief that it improves lives or enhances a customer experience, is thought of as something you would use or recommend to loved ones, and is given a fair shot, then it is likely to be a game-changing success. If, after all that, the innovation fails, that is still okay, as it will result in real learning and keep the innovative spirit alive within the organization.

Remember, good ideas are a dime a dozen, and great ideas are laughed at. Putting on today's lens to solve tomorrow's problems is the single biggest barrier to innovation. Just because you don't see the possibilities with someone else's innovation does not mean they are not there.

# CHAPTER 7

# The Networked Development of Innovation

**In the 1920s—the era of big band music**—the advent of commercial music recording and the growing popularity of the radio were making the guitar an increasingly irrelevant musical instrument. Guitars just weren't loud enough to compete with the larger and louder instruments, especially with the drums and brass section of a band. So the guitar was relegated to smaller performances and venues where the sound could be heard. Clearly, a louder guitar was needed. Many solutions were attempted, such as a larger size, steel strings, and even a metal body. A phonograph-like amplifying horn attached to the guitar was even proposed. But it was the combination of electricity and music that reinvented the guitar and made it the most prolific instrument in Western music today.

Two innovators, musician and vaudeville performer George Beauchamp and engineer Adolph Rickenbacker, invented an electromagnetic device that picked up the vibrations of the guitar strings and converted them to electric signals, which were then amplified and played through speakers.[20] This invention resulted in a lap guitar that was called *the frying pan* because it looked like one. And while the frying pan guitar faded, the pickup device Beauchamp and Rickenbacker developed was the true revolutionary invention. Although Beauchamp and Rickenbacker were the first to invent the guitar pickup, the idea of using electricity to amplify the sound of string instruments was old news; they built on existing knowledge to create something new and valuable to society.

Once the idea of the electromagnetic pickup was known, innovations in the electric guitar started piling on from all directions. The pickup was adapted to the traditional Spanish guitar, with a hollow body. Soon after, a solid-body guitar was developed, as were other variations. The guitar went from six strings to ten or twelve strings and from one neck to two; inventors created just about every other combination or design that could be dreamed up. The innovations came from a collaboration of musicians, engineers, and entrepreneurs, each one building on the other. This was truly networked progress.

The networked development of the electric guitar didn't end with variations in guitars and sounds. This instrument catalyzed a new generation of music called rock and roll. Between the mid-1950s

---

20  Theodoros II, "How the Electric Guitar Was Invented," *Gizmodo* (October 29, 2013), http://gizmodo.com/how-the-electric-guitar-was-invented-1453939129.

and the mid-1960s, millions of electric guitars were sold, giving popularity to a sound that would last generations.

## Nothing new under the sun

The single common theme of every innovation is that they always build on other ideas. Nothing is out of the blue. Nothing is independent. Progress breeds progress. Improvements lead to other improvements. Innovations are networked, just like the Internet—everything is connected. Creativity and innovation are about improving on what is out there and connecting dots in an original way to create new value.

This book is one example of ideas building on existing ideas. Most of the stories on innovation in this book have been retold countless times. This book is an attempt to understand and classify commonalties across these innovations into themes that will, hopefully, provide practical value for developing future innovations.

Innovations are rarely, if ever, unique breakthroughs with no history. They come from interconnected, networked ideas. They come from expanding on the lessons of the past. The one common truth is that if an innovation had not happened as it did, it would still have happened with a different set of players and circumstances. We would still have antibiotics if Alexander Fleming had not observed that mold kills bacteria. We would still have made the same advances in organic chemistry had Kekulé not dreamed of a serpent biting its tail. And electric guitars would be just as popular if Beauchamp and Rickenbacker had not invented the first electromagnetic guitar pickup.

In fact, most innovations are developed simultaneously by multiple innovators. Mark Lemley's insightful 2012 paper[21] highlights the fact that almost all major technologies are invented simultaneously or near simultaneously by two or more teams working independently of each other. He goes on to argue that there are two key elements in his theory of innovations. First, inventions are not a discontinuity; they are incremental steps and are heavily based on extensions of existing knowledge. Second, invention by one person or group is exceedingly rare, and rarely does an inventor come up with an idea that no one else is working on. These elements apply not only to smaller innovations but also to the big breakthroughs that today we consider some of the greatest inventions in history.

Take the lightbulb, for example. Thomas Edison is the individual credited for its invention. But while Edison commercialized the use of the lightbulb and created a successful cluster of value for electric lighting, the lightbulb was invented decades before Edison got involved. There were over 20 inventors of incandescent lamps prior to Edison's version.[22] While the older bulbs had a short lifespan, Edison's lightbulb improved the filament to give his lamps a meaningful and useful lifespan. His bamboo-based filament could last up to twelve-hundred hours.

The story of simultaneous invention and networked improvement is repeated over and over. The telegraph, the airplane, the

---

21  Mark A. Lemley, "The Myth of the Sole Inventor," *Michigan Law Review*, vol. 110 (2012), http://repository.law.umich.edu/cgi/viewcontent.cgi?article=1125 &context=mlr.
22  Bulbs.com, "History of the Light Bulb," http://www.bulbs.com/learning/history. aspx.

automobile, and almost every innovation we can think of has gone through this process.

Networked development also happens when a discovery in one field makes a breakthrough in another field possible. The invention of the telegraph, the first major breakthrough in electronic communication, depended on earlier developments, such as Alessandro Volta's invention of the battery in 1800 (which reliably stored electric current) and the relationship between electricity and magnetism shown by Dutch physicist Hans Christian Oersted in 1820.

## Keep your eyes peeled

In some cases, an innovation is on hold, waiting for the right circumstances before it blossoms. The history of innovation is littered with discoveries that go through periods of dormancy. They gather dust until unrelated developments appear and revive their progress. Contact lenses, for example, are one of the biggest innovations in corrective vision. However, even after the concept of lenses covering the eye was shown to be feasible and effective, the idea of contact lenses stayed dormant for sixty years because it was impractical to make molds of sensitive corneal tissue. Decades later, after anesthesia was invented—an unrelated development in another field—contact lens technology gained new life because getting molds of corneal tissue was now possible.

Networked improvement also suggests that it is always useful to be on the lookout for new developments. Many developments are shared and known but ignored until the next player comes onto the scene and picks up progress and creates value. Returning to the story of Alexander Fleming's serendipitous discovery in 1928 of penicillin's antibacterial properties, Fleming knew he had made a monumental discovery. People with infections were dying for lack of a cure. Fleming published his findings in 1929. But his discovery lay dormant for a decade, until another group of scientists (Howard Florey and Ernst Chain) came upon his work, built upon it, and created a practical use for penicillin in treating people suffering from bacterial infections. How much did society suffer during that decade? This opportunity had been identified and was simply waiting for someone to create untold value for society and untold riches for themselves. How many more of these opportunities are out there?

## Collaborate

It is a well-known fact that human creativity is enhanced through idea sharing and interaction. Innovations aren't typically generated by genius inventors who toil alone in a dusky lab. Innovation thrives when ideas are shared. Studies have shown that increases in population density lead to a greater rate of idea generation, productivity, and economic output. Cities are where innovation happens, and this is primarily due to the increased opportunities to exchange ideas.[23] The ability to share ideas and build innovation networks is the reason innovation is localized. Silicon Valley and my native Seattle have become the hotbeds for technology innovation, while other large cities around the country and world have

---

23  Steven Johnson, *Where Good Ideas Come From* (Riverhead, 2011).

become hotbeds for innovation in automobiles, banking, financial services, and other industries.

Throughout history, collaboration has been key to driving innovation. Steve Jobs, regarded by many as the most brilliant innovator of our generation, was a consummate collaborator who was adept at getting feedback on ideas from a diverse set of people. He said, "When a good idea comes, you know, part of my job is to move it around, just see what different people think, get people talking about it, argue with people about it, get ideas moving."[24]

Corporations are the equivalent of cities, populated by people with vastly diverse experiences and ideas that can all lead to creativity. Networking and the sharing of ideas are constant across functions and departments in innovative organizations; if they are not in yours, they need to be encouraged. Many breakthroughs continue to happen within large corporations. Some examples include, the first digital camera was developed at Kodak, the first computer mouse at Xerox, the first modern-day electric car at GM, and the original smartphone at Nokia. Breakthrough innovation happens within corporations, just not often enough—and when it does, companies often do not recognize its potential. Idea sharing and networked development is the backbone of innovation, and it is essential to create an environment where this happens.

---

24  Betsy Morris, "Steve Jobs Speaks Out," *Fortune* (March 7, 2008), http://archive.fortune.com/galleries/2008/fortune/0803/gallery.jobsqna.fortune/7.html.

# CHAPTER 8

# Clusters of Value

**When we walk down the endless aisles of** frozen foods at Trader Joe's or Whole Foods or virtually any supermarket in the world, we never stop to wonder how food, frozen a long time ago, can stay fresh and (reasonably) tasty. Clarence Birdseye's name probably does not come to mind when you think about the great innovators in history. He is credited with the invention of frozen foods and was the most prominent facilitator of today's frozen food industry. While living in Canada in the 1910s during one of his many fur-trapping excursions, Birdseye, a New Yorker, noticed that fish stayed fresh longer if it was frozen right after it was caught. And it tasted better when thawed and eaten months later. The key insight that revolutionized the concept of frozen foods was that flash freezing—freezing food immediately and quickly and keeping it frozen until you were ready to cook it—allowed it to retain its freshness for a long time.

Frozen foods were available long before Birdseye made his observation, but they were frozen slowly and failed to retain their original textures and tastes. And, really, no one wanted to eat them. Additionally, food was not frozen in quantities that consumers could use; there were no individual or family sizes.

Birdseye sought to change that, and to do so, he built an entire interconnected system of activities and equipment to popularize and bring great-tasting frozen foods to the public. He developed the logistics of freezing foods quickly and at the right temperature through his quick-freeze machine. He had to develop packaging to keep the food frozen and safe. There was no way at the time to transport copious amounts of frozen food, so he introduced insulated railroad cars. To keep his food frozen at the store, he developed the refrigerated grocery-display cases we still use today. By some counts, he had 168 patents related to frozen foods.

Using today's terminology, Birdseye developed an entire ecosystem or cluster of value that enabled the popularization of frozen foods. His invention was not simply the flash-freezing method or machine; it was the entire cluster of related developments that made frozen foods wildly and increasingly successful for almost a century. Today, over a quarter of a trillion dollars of frozen foods are sold annually.

Throughout history, many of the largest and most successful innovators have developed a strong ecosystem that lets an innovation shine. This cluster of value is a bundle of interconnected systems, products, companies, technologies, government agencies, and other organizations that collectively benefit an innovation and help it succeed. These value clusters are not built for collusion or to create competitive barriers (although they may do that quite effectively). They are built to enhance the value of the innovation. Without the right support structure or cluster of value, innovations have a lower probability of becoming breakthroughs.

The first cluster of innovation value in history may be the one built around the wheel. We have already seen that the axle was a critical part of the success of the wheel. In addition, the wheel without roads is not valuable. Even after its invention, the wheel took a step back and gave way to the camel in the deserts of the Middle East and northern Africa, because roads were hard to build and camels were a better mode of transport—they were less likely to get stuck in the sand.

Since the introduction of the first electric arc lamp in 1802 by English inventor Humphry Davy, inventors tried to make a practical lightbulb that could be used in homes. For decades, many people tried to make a better product, a better lightbulb. They worked on the technical aspects, most notably on how to make the filament last longer. Thomas Edison worked on this as well. His team's breakthrough, after testing over six thousand variations, was inventing a filament made of carbonized bamboo that, as we discussed earlier, lasted over twelve-hundred hours—far longer than anything else. However, what made Edison's lightbulb successful was the fact that he also thought about the entire cluster of value—not just selling the lightbulbs but creating an end-to-end commercially viable system for electric lighting. His vision was to make electric lighting affordable to everybody. In fact, he was famously reported to have said, "We will make electric light so cheap that only the rich will be able to burn candles."[25]

Edison built the entire suite of products that made the light-bulb usable, scalable, and practical, including the distribution of electricity from a central generator, the methodology to track how much electricity each consumer is using (the electric meter), and the first commercial power utility. It was this cluster of value that enabled Edison's lightbulb to become the standard.

The Segway is a perfect example of a fantastic invention without the supporting cluster of value. In 2001, after a year of secrecy and building anticipation, the supposedly greatest machine on earth was unveiled. It was one of the most high-profile product launches ever. The Segway was supposed to be to the automobile what the automobile had been to the horse and buggy. It was accompanied by colossal expectations and was touted to be bigger than the Internet. It had all the mindshare, resources, and attention required to become great.

As most of us know now, sales of the Segway ended up being a tiny fraction of what was expected. In the end, it became a case study for how *not* to launch a product. The company, Segway, was recently sold to a Chinese investor, presumably for a fraction of its earlier value.

The Segway was a great invention. The technology was something the world had never seen, allowing the user to practically move by thought. But it just did not have the supporting

---

25 Queens Borough Public Library, "Thomas A. Edison, 1884" (2017), http://edison.rutgers.edu/latimer/tae1.htm.

infrastructure, the cluster of value that was required to make it mainstream. No one was sure if you were supposed to use it on the road or the sidewalk. It was too slow to be on the street and too fast to be safe among pedestrians. How should insurance companies deal with it; do you need auto coverage? The lack of a strong supporting cluster of value was one of the main reasons why the Segway failed to succeed in the market, unlike Clarence Birdseye's frozen foods or Edison's lightbulb.

Great innovations almost always rely on a cluster of supporting inventions—an ecosystem to help them thrive. The greater the innovation's impact on society, the greater the need for a cluster of value that supports it. Without the supporting cluster of value, a brilliant invention may just fall by the wayside. My advice to corporations who are looking for breakthroughs is to always think about an innovation broadly and determine whether all the supporting elements needed to make it successful are in place. If not, build it yourself, like Birdseye and Edison did.

# CHAPTER 9

# The Environment to Catalyze Innovation

**Over a thousand years ago, centuries before paper** currency was used anywhere else in the world, at a time when monetary value was determined by the weight of gold and precious jewels, emperor Kublai Khan of the Yuan dynasty in China mandated the use of paper money for all transactions. Anyone who did not accept the government's printed pieces of paper as legal tender faced death.

Italian explorer Marco Polo was stunned when he visited China and saw merchants from neighboring regions bring in real valuables like gold, rubies, and expensive ornaments to exchange them with the emperor's staff for . . . paper! He observed that a stack of these pieces of paper weighed only a fraction of a gold coin. Equally stunning was that citizens could buy anything they wanted all over the empire with these pieces of paper. People could also go to the emperor anytime and exchange valuables for paper. Pretty soon, all the riches in the empire (all the gold in Fort Knox?) belonged to the emperor, and the citizens had nothing more than pieces of paper. But commerce still proceeded effectively. When Polo returned to Europe and shared his observations, this practice was met with extreme disbelief. Who in their right mind would give up gold for pieces of paper?

Today, we are having the same discussion, the same incredulousness, with a new form of digital currency: bitcoin. We are asking the same questions about bitcoin that the erudite citizens asked about paper currency a thousand years ago. Time will tell whether bitcoin or other forms of digital money will be as popular as paper currency, but today's reaction to a brand-new form of monetary value makes us appreciate how people must have felt about paper currency centuries ago.

Historically, the emperor's mandate facilitated acceptance of the innovation (and, of course, the pain of death is a powerful incentive). Regardless, citizens found value. They were always paid a generous price, and everyone was able to conduct transactions fairly and get whatever they needed with nothing more than pieces of paper.

Although this example happened centuries ago, it demonstrates the adoption of an innovation through a created environment that allowed the breakthrough to succeed. In this case, it happened through a vision established and enforced uniformly by the leader. Emperor Kublai Kahn established a vision and implemented it consistently. The benefits of the system were clear, and there were severe consequences to those who deviated. Today, the details and techniques could be different, but the fundamental philosophy that the environment can make or break an innovation still applies.

The environment has always been influential in determining the success or failure of an innovation. The environment includes the external factors, sociopolitical conditions, parallel developments, and everything else that allows an innovation to shine. At the most fundamental level, capitalism has been a more prolific innovation environment than socialism. The environment can affect the outcome of an innovation in many ways. Sometimes one development provides the environment that lets another innovation thrive. For example, previously we covered the stories of two independent innovations: the microwave oven and frozen foods. These two developments are linked, as it was the emergence of the first that catalyzed the adoption of the second. Frozen foods were still a novelty until World War II, when canned foods had to be rationed because tin was scarce. Frozen food, the cheap and available alternative, got a huge boost as a result. The boost from World War II and the new availability of the microwave oven created an environment conducive to the widespread adoption of frozen foods.

World War II also resulted in an immense lift in another innovation we discussed earlier. During the war, the military didn't have enough penicillin to treat the wounded. Companies like Glaxo and Pfizer started creating penicillin in significant quantities for the war, resulting in untold value in terms of lives saved. The mass production of penicillin and antibiotics has reportedly saved well over 200 million lives to date. In this case, the war was an environmental factor that tangibly demonstrated the societal value of the drug, resulting in the broad acceptance of an innovation—penicillin.

ATMs used to be large, clunky machines, and people did not trust a machine to manage their cash when they had the option to choose a smiling bank teller who knew them by name. ATMs gained in popularity, aided by both macro- and microenablers. The macroenabler was the stage of development of society. The late 1960s and 1970s was the time when self-service became more mainstream, so people were becoming accustomed to using machines for many different transactions. John Shepherd-Barron, the Scotsman credited with the invention of the ATM, had his flash of insight one day when an idea popped into his mind: If a vending machine can dispense a chocolate bar, why can't it dispense cash? (In fact, just like Archimedes, this eureka moment hit him while he was in the bathtub.) In the US, ATMs gained popularity through the microenvironment. When a 1978 snowstorm in New York paralyzed the city and shut down banks, people had to get money from somewhere. ATMs—open all the time—were the solution.

Timing is, indeed, everything. Innovations have been launched before their time and failed, and being too late is never a good idea. It is prudent to stay aware of the macro trends; they often guide the development of new experiences. Part of having a prepared mind is the keen sense of what is going on around you and how to take advantage of the environment.

Today, software is reshaping almost every industry. Companies are either using software to disrupt or getting disrupted by software. This is the environment we are living in, and it would be wise to have a thorough understanding of how software can alter your customer's experience. AI may be the biggest environmental disruptor over the coming decade, and companies need to be prepared to thrive in an AI world. The next broad trend could be something that we can't dream up today, but the fact that will always be true is that the environment will play a crucial role in the success of an innovation.

# PART 3

---

# IMPLEMENTING THE INNOVATION BIOME

**From the previous chapters, we now have a** good idea of the attributes that impact and drive innovation. We know innovation requires a primed mind and a network of knowledge transfer. We have learned that conventional wisdom consistently proves to be an inhibitor or distractor and is something we should be mindful of as we engage in the creation of high-value offerings. We know innovation is collaborative and includes an interconnected ecosystem, a cluster of value. And, finally, we know the role of the environment is critical to the success of a new development.

To increase the rate of corporate innovation, your organization needs to encourage these innovation catalysts. On your quest for innovation, a framework or conceptual model that fosters innovation is indispensable. Without a framework, innovation simply becomes a shot in the dark. This situation holds many companies back from innovation today.

A good innovation framework should build on existing knowledge, provide an underlying theory to guide activities, and deliver the tools and knowledge necessary to drive innovation forward in a systematic and replicable manner. The framework should highlight the activities your company will engage in to let the innovation attributes thrive; as a result, you'll develop a healthy innovation biome. Within a healthy and productive setting, innovation becomes a habit, something unconscious and constant. While individual inventors will continue to drive innovation, the only thing companies and corporate executives can do is provide the necessary conditions and circumstances for innovation to happen.

I've created a framework you can use to create a productive innovation biome. It involves three steps, detailed in the next three chapters.

# CHAPTER 10

# The CARE Model

**The CARE model is an approach that will** help your corporation create an innovation biome. It describes the types of innovation opportunities within an organization and matches specific activities with them to maximize their potential.

The CARE model was inspired by the work of Dr. Douglas Engelbart,[26] one of the most thoughtful and creative minds in the development of the computer and the Internet. He introduced the concepts of collective IQ and networked improvement communities. According to Dr. Engelbart, an *improvement community* is any group involved in a collective pursuit to improve a given capability. While all improvement communities drive innovation, a

---

26  Douglas Engelbart, "Improving Our Ability to Improve: A Call for Investment in a New Future," IBM Co-Evolution Symposium (2003).

community that puts special attention on how it can solve important problems more effectively and that boosts its collective IQ by employing better tools and practices in innovative and collaborative ways is a *networked improvement community*. Networked improvement communities are used across disciplines to improve the innovation capabilities and outcomes of large and complex initiatives, notably in the field of education and health care services.

I have taken the liberty of building on Dr. Engelbart's work, which involves organizing corporate activities into distinct buckets, by introducing the CARE model, a systematic way for companies to get a thorough view of their innovation activities and to develop a methodology that provides the matching set of tools for various innovation activities.

Companies engage in four activities to further their mission. Everything your company does falls into one of these four buckets:

- Core
- Advancement
- Reframing
- Experiential

Core activities are the ongoing business functions of the organization, the day-to-day activities required to stay in business. They include the activities that need to be done every day, such as manufacturing, marketing, sales, distribution, finance, and any other activity needed to keep the lights running and the bills paid. For example, building and selling mobile phones, sedans, antihypertensives, or bottles of cleaning supplies all fall into this bucket (assuming you are, respectively, a mobile phone manufacturer, car manufacturer, pharmaceutical company, or chemical household goods manufacturer).

Advancement activities are any improvements made to the core activities. Improving products by adding features, enhancing customer support, and increasing efficiency are simple examples. Developing the next generation of your mobile phone or sedan, and improving product quality or the efficiency of the manufacturing process are advancement activities.

Reframing activities involve creating something new by doing things in an entirely new way. Since reframing activities require looking at problems through an entirely new lens or with a different frame of reference, most R&D activities and much of the basic research within companies, government, and university labs fall into this bucket. For example, the invention of the Internet and robotic surgery, and most new advances driven by original research, fall into this category.

Finally, experiential activities use existing knowledge to create new products and approaches with the goal of enhancing human experiences and creating new customer value. These activities include connecting dots and combining available knowledge and technology to create a new way of interacting with them. So, while the invention of the Internet may be considered a reframing activity, the application of the Internet to shopping or banking is an experiential activity.

The activities in the CARE model do not represent a continuum. They are discrete and primarily distinguished by what you are trying to achieve in your innovation efforts. To summarize, with advancement activities, you are improving on something you are already doing (your core activities); with reframing activities, you are inventing something brand new; and with experiential activities, you are bringing new customer value to the world by creatively connecting available components and knowledge.

Mapping your improvement and innovation activities along these dimensions is the first step to understanding your own innovation process. Which categories are you currently implementing in your company? Which ones *should* you implement to better capitalize on your market and to create the type of innovation you want for your organization? If you don't understand your own innovation process, you are not going to be able to innovate efficiently.

By definition, core activities lack innovation; they are simply focused on execution, so we won't spend any more time on them. All innovation happens at the advancement, reframing, or experiential level. Each of these three sets of activities can result in outcomes of any size, and there is no single type that is better or more desirable than the others. While people are often tempted to only think about developing breakthroughs, it is important to realize that activities in each of these buckets enhance societal value. An advancement innovation, for example, can be far more impactful than an innovation created through reframing or experiential activities (or vice versa). The key point to keep in mind is that each type of innovation requires a different approach and a distinct set of tools.

## Advancement activities

Advancement activities lead to incremental innovation, because they improve your current products or processes. Incremental innovations are critical for improving products, extending and expanding the product line, gaining market share, and increasing profits. The majority of the world's innovations are incremental; this is the life-blood of a company. A healthy investment in advancement activities is essential to keep your products and services relevant for a long time. A lack of advancement activities results in the loss of satisfied customers and market share. The outcome of advancement activities will rarely result in a radically different customer experience, but they are critical to maintaining and growing your core business.

Making your product better, enhancing the customer experience, developing products for new markets, expanding the audience, developing line extensions, creating more efficient processes, and reducing costs are all designed to improve or advance what you are already doing. Advancement activities, such as the stepped increases in computer processing speed or the number of blades on your razor, give you satisfied customers and drive the arms race between competitors. They allow you to become more efficient in building products and managing processes, making your company more profitable or leading to lower prices or better features. Advancement activities will not require any real changes to your company's business model, but without them, we would still be driving Model Ts or playing golf with a 3-wood that was actually made of wood.

To be successful at incremental innovation, it is important to be clear about its characteristics and the advancement tools used for it. As an example, let's take the development of the next model of a sedan. The first thing to understand is that the problem set must be well defined. You know you are working on next year's model of the automobile. That's it. While advancement activities can and should have a broad impact on your company's performance, the problem set is narrow: improving the core activity of building and selling your current line of cars. You know—without ambiguity— the outcome will be a sedan that's noticeably improved but still basically the same car. This is your research question, the equation you want to solve, and you have just defined what you are solving.

Next, the set of improvements—as well as how you'll implement those improvements—must be designed before you begin to work on them. In effect, you create an improvement plan first and then work toward achieving the plan, something most companies routinely do. You plan out the next version of your product—new safety features, a slightly modified silhouette—and then execute on it. Never start the advancement activity without a plan in place. Sure, there will be hiccups along the way, and things will often not go according to plan. Maybe a new braking system is delayed at the component manufacturer, or you have to redesign a new part. You will make course corrections, but the idea is to execute on the plan you have developed.

For most advancement activities, the solutions are predetermined and then implemented—you don't figure it out as you go. For example, if your sedan requires a third-party component, the decision on what vendor to use is made first. Usually, multiple solutions or ideas are not implemented in the hope of seeing which one succeeds. You would never consider implementing two different stereo systems or navigation systems to determine which one works better. In this type of activity, you evaluate options, pick one, and implement it.

The primary activity for advancement is analysis. You listen to customer feedback, conduct market research, understand what your competitors are doing, and increasingly use data and analytics to power innovation at this level. The capabilities that the world of data analytics and customer research provide us are designed for advancement. Because the problem set is well defined, the tools are also well defined. We know how to measure the drivers of satisfaction and develop customer lifetime-value models, manage competitive intelligence, and deploy any of the countless techniques that help us analyze customers, competitors, and market trends.

Organizationally, advancement is best done within a single group, under a single set of priorities. For example, there is usually one team responsible for designing and building the next generation of an automobile.

Finally, if there is a stall in advancement activities, the logical approach is to break up the problem into smaller and smaller components. If you are stuck or unsure of which direction to go, you narrow down the problem set, try to pinpoint with surgical precision where improvements are necessary, and then start making the necessary improvements. This is one of the fundamental characteristics of analytics-driven innovation.

Advancement activities are best evaluated by the common metrics of business and market performance, including revenue and profit growth, customer satisfaction, market share, efficiency improvement, and other improvement metrics.

## Reframing activities

Reframing activities create a new capability or a new way of doing things, which can lead to breakthrough innovation—something new, without precedent. These are the types of activities that spawn the creation of altogether new industries. Examples of rethinking or reframing activities include the invention of the automobile, the airplane, television, penicillin, the Internet, and electric vehicles.

The development of the Internet is one of the greatest reframing developments in recent memory. It was developed through collaboration, idea sharing, and networked improvement. It includes all the attributes of the innovation process we have learned thus far. Unlike an advancement activity, the Internet was not an improvement on something that was already out there. It was designed by a group of pioneers working independently across universities and research institutions around the world. The development of the Internet was driven by the people who comprehended the possibilities inherent in different technological advances and by a common desire to have individual computers connected to one another. It required a level of information sharing and collaboration that would be hard to achieve within today's competitive corporate environment, and its development was guided by a *shared belief* that was adopted voluntarily by a diverse set of innovators who shared a common goal.

The biggest difference between reframing activities and advancement activities is that the reframing level's problem is broad, and the outcome is undefined. This is the opposite mindset from the incremental, analytics-based advancement activities we just discussed. Unlike an advancement activity, such as the development of the next model of a sedan, a reframing activity often has a broader or, in some cases, undefined goal. No one really knew the shape the Internet would take before it was developed. At the reframing level of activity, you'd be thinking about entirely new ways of doing things—such as developing an electric car, which could make the previous gas model obsolete—rather than improved customer satisfaction, market share, or profits. This process may also be described as *discontinuous* or *nonlinear* innovation.

The tools used for successful reframing activities differ from the analytics-driven tools that are so effective for advancement activities. Since the scope is broad and the solution is undefined, the best way to innovate at the reframing level is through networked improvement communities. These are communities or teams that work independently but collaboratively, boosting the collective IQ of all involved in the innovation. As we just saw, the development of the Internet was a loose collaboration by independent pioneers scattered across different organizations.

Networked improvement communities require a shared goal or a focus on a common area of interest, and they usually have multiple people working, often independently, toward developing solutions to achieve that goal. The communities, while diverse, need to operate with discipline, agree to share progress with others, and use what is learned from each other. This is what boosts the collective knowledge of all participants and gets the entire community closer to achieving the shared goal. This is how breakthroughs are more likely to occur.

In the corporate environment, this structure can be created and replicated, and success can be achieved in reframing activities when multiple teams work independently but share developments and collaborate. Having multiple teams work on a broad area gives you better odds of success than having a single team working on it. And because there is no fixed solution, any number of paths can lead to a breakthrough. The key, however, is to encourage collaboration and idea sharing. Networked improvement is most likely to thrive at these idea-sharing sessions and thus advance the shared agenda of all participants.

Understanding the differences between advancement and reframing activities can help resolve a common pain point faced by many large organizations. When corporate executives audit innovation or new development activities across their organization, they often find multiple and separate teams working in the same broad area. And each team is often asking for more resources to be successful. The logical reaction by the executives is to propose consolidation of these disparate teams into one; that way, there is a larger dedicated unit to solve the problem, and success is more likely because there is more wood behind the arrow. Additionally, most executives would reason that, since the consolidated team has enough critical mass, no one needs additional budgetary or head-count resources.

Before making such a decision, you would be well advised to understand the type of activity the teams are trying to solve. If they are working on advancement activities, it makes perfect sense to consolidate the disparate efforts into a unified one, as these activities involve developing and executing a single approach. On the other hand, for reframing activities—which are best served by networked improvement—it may be better to have multiple and parallel teams working independently but also collaboratively, with regular progress sharing among them to encourage the best solution to emerge.

We also learned that whenever you reach a dead end in advancement activities, a good approach in developing a solution is to narrow the problem into smaller components and work on them.

In reframing activities, the opposite approach is true: When you reach an impasse, often the better approach is to move up a level of abstraction. Question the problem itself, and question whether you are on the right track, and you might find that solutions and breakthroughs emerge as you tackle a larger issue. Since reframing activities often advance a science, they are best served by precompetitive or collaborative efforts. The development of the Internet is a prime example of a *precompetitive development.* In this case, information and developments were freely and broadly shared across organizations, and information sharing was not inhibited for competitive reasons. Companies are warming to the idea of shared innovation at a precompetitive level (such as Facebook's Open Compute Project). While the approach should make all boats rise, a significant portion of original research and reframing activities still happen within government and university settings, where competition is less ingrained in the culture.

## Experiential activities

Experiential activities inspire experiential innovation. The starting point for these activities is altering and enhancing human experiences. Experiential activities are less about the original research and more about the possibilities created with what is available. While advancement activities improve an existing offering and reframing activities create entirely new approaches and developments, experiential activities are about connecting the dots. Here is where you convert your reframing or any other developments into offerings or products that alter human experiences.

For example, creating the Internet was a reframing activity, but using the Internet to alter the shopping experience or the way you consume books and music is an experiential activity. The discovery and invention of penicillin was not experiential, but using penicillin to save the lives of millions of people is. Experiential innovation is not about making a better phone or camera but about the new experiences that are created when the two are in a single device. Inventing the automobile or the airplane is a reframing activity, but using these innovations to redefine how billions of people travel alters travelers' experiences forever.

This may sound like circular reasoning, but it is crucial to understand. Transformational innovations are best achieved through experiential activities, since they fundamentally alter experiences. Experiential activities are often an extension of reframing or other experiential activities. For example, the Internet and the proliferation of mobile technology have led to many experiential developments. In turn, these experiential innovations and applications have led to further proliferation of these technologies, leading to even more experience-altering innovations.

The tools required for experiential innovation are slightly different from those required for advancement and reframing activities. Experiential activities require the following tools:

- A deep understanding of domain knowledge, as well as associated developments in parallel domains
- The ability to synthesize available knowledge and know-how
- A clear understanding of the experience journey you are trying to alter

- The ability to develop a better experience using, working from, and synthesizing available technology and knowledge

In the next chapter, we will highlight in detail the tools and approaches that make experiential innovation a reality through the development of experience journeys. But for now, let's look at how the CARE model applies to corporate innovation.

## The CARE model in action

The following table summarizes the CARE model characteristics:

| Activity | Definition | Skills and tools | Type of innovation | Ideal setting |
|---|---|---|---|---|
| Core | Managing core activities | Execution | | |
| Advancement | Improving on core activities | Analysis | Incremental | Competitive |
| Reframing | Creating new inventions | Networked improvement | Breakthrough | Precompetitive |
| Experiential | Creating new experiences using available knowledge | Experience journeys | Transformational | Competitive |

Large companies are good at core and advancement activities. This is how they have maintained their success and relevance in the market. They operate their core activities with high efficiency. They have established tools to create better products and services (advancement activities). And they really understand how to improve their offerings by gaining insights from customers, competitors, and market trends. In fact, being so good at these activities creates a common fear that their sound business practices may prevent them from offering the next generation of value to customers.

In the first chapter, we looked at the Kodak example, a company so efficient at core and advancement activities and so adamant about maintaining that trend that it found it hard to accept the reframing developments altering its business. The core activity was selling lucrative rolls of film, and the advancement activities were the investments it was making to sell more rolls of film. When Steven Sasson invented the digital camera, it was an entirely new product and approach—a reframing activity. The company found it hard to incorporate this reframing innovation into its existing business model, which was overwhelmingly focused on being successful in core and advancement activities.

Most large corporations do invest heavily in reframing activities. They have large R&D departments, but the jury is still out regarding how effective these activities are. Yes, a lot of patents are granted (approximately 325,000 annually) and ideas are developed, but how many of them have translated into offerings that enhance societal value?

Startups are particularly good at experiential activities that result in transformational innovation. They don't have the vast resources required for original research but are good at piecing together new experiences from existing technology and knowledge. Large companies can do this effectively, but they typically don't have an established experiential innovation function. By this I mean a function that takes existing developments (from within and outside the company) and creates brand-new experiences with them. They have sensing and insight teams that stay abreast and update the organization on trends, R&D teams that push the boundaries of science, and product teams that are experts in core and advancement activities, but they do not have anything dedicated to innovation through new experiences. This is a gaping hole that needs to be filled to create the transformational innovation corporations are hungry for.

## When to compete and when to collaborate

As discussed earlier, most of us would agree that the iPhone is a great innovation that has dramatically altered how we communicate and consume information and has given us a seemingly endless source of utility and enjoyment.

Using our innovation taxonomy, the iPhone is a successful experiential innovation. At the time of its development, most of the components and technologies that make up the iPhone had been available for everyone to use. The true genius of the offering was in putting existing components and functionality together into a beautiful, useful, and experience-transforming package that millions of people lined up to buy. The cluster of value was also, in itself, true genius: The offering consisted of the entire set of developments, which included the actual physical device, the connection with mobile networks (starting with an exclusive relationship with AT&T), the pricing model, and the entire ecosystem of partners and app developers. The market result of this innovation was that it ran circles around its competitors. Apple has sold over a billion iPhones, leading it to become the most valuable company on earth.

The interesting thing about the iPhone is that almost all of the breakthroughs that made it special, including the touch screen, GPS, Internet, and cellular technology, were developed at the precompetitive level. In fact, these breakthroughs were developed either by the government or through government-funded research. This topic is well researched and covered in Mariana Mazzucato's book *The Entrepreneurial State.*[27] The following figure summarizes the government-funded innovations that went into the iPod and iPhone.

# Who Puts the "Smart" in a Smart Phone?

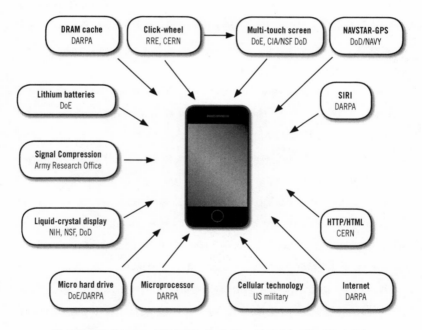

Adapted from *The Entrepreneurial State: Debunking Public vs. Private Sector Myths* (2015, p.116)

---

27  Mariana Mazzucato, *The Entrepreneurial State* (Hachette, 2015).

Precompetitive collaboration is the sharing or joint conducting of research or developments by companies that ordinarily compete. It also includes developments done before getting to a commercially competitive level. This includes work done within government or university settings, or a collaborative effort between companies and universities or governments.

The US government spent approximately $145 billion in 2016 on R&D—a staggering sum. This includes basic research in just about every area, including medicine, smart cities, cybersecurity, sustainable energy, the Internet of Things, agriculture, housing, transportation, education, space exploration, and numerous other areas. The basic research that has been done over the decades has shaped our lives. How we travel, communicate, fight diseases, live, and use many of the comforts we enjoy every day have their roots in basic research done at the precompetitive level.

Of the three innovation activities we have discussed, the overall impact to societal value will be greatest if advancement and experiential activities occur at the competitive level and reframing activities happen at a precompetitive level.

Advancement activities that drive incremental innovation must be competitive. This is what gives customers the best offerings at the best prices. Competition is the natural order that keeps companies innovating and improving.

Reframing activities, on the other hand, rely on basic research. This is best done through an open and collaborative approach. Competition and exclusivity of ideas are detrimental and likely to slow down advancement. Additionally, since reframing activities are best served by idea sharing, collaboration, and networked improvement, precompetitive efforts such as government and university research, or joint efforts between companies or the private and public sectors, are likely to offer greater odds of success.

Experiential activities are best done at a competitive level. Companies have an economic incentive to provide the best experience to customers, and they should be free to take all available knowledge from their own developments or the public domain and build transformational offerings. Building an experiential capability is a competitive advantage. We just saw how Apple has reaped the rewards from an experiential innovation, as have many other innovative companies. The companies that build the best experiential innovation capabilities will have the biggest rewards.

## Activity-level targets

To build a biome where all three types of innovations can flourish, it is essential to ensure you have the right set of activities at each level. The first step is to develop a list of major activities performed within your organization and classify them according to each of the four activity types. This exercise will provide a clear understanding of what innovation efforts are going on within your company. If all of your innovation efforts are analysis-driven and focused on making products and processes better, you're focused solely on advancement of your core business. There is nothing wrong with that, and it can lead to a successful enterprise for a long time. However, this approach is unlikely to drive the creation of breakthroughs or transformations and is consistently going to result in incremental innovation. If you and your management team want to create the next generation of value, you need to ensure you include a sufficient number of reframing and experiential activities in your innovation plan to get you to your goal. Without knowledge of the activities in place, you will simply gamble on innovation efforts with a faint hope of a payoff.

The next step is setting effort targets for each activity. These may vary based on your priorities and your business. Highly R&D-oriented companies may have a higher investment (people and dollars) in reframing activities, whereas other companies may invest more heavily in advancement and experiential activities. Here's a good place to start:

- Core activities get 50 percent of corporate effort.
- Advancement activities get 30 percent of corporate effort.
- Reframing activities get 10 percent of corporate effort.
- Experiential activities get 10 percent of corporate effort.

Your corporate effort includes budget, time, energy, and priority. If you do establish goals for these activities, it is important to follow through. This means actually spending the time, energy, effort, and dollars on each of them. The effort needs to be specific to the desired activities. If your goal is experiential innovation, the effort must translate to working on activities that alter experiences and not on advancement or reframing activities.

Don't squander your resources on the wrong activities. Embrace your potential for innovation and then invest in the right path to make it happen.

# CHAPTER 11

# The Experience Delta

**As I was writing this section of the book,** I was pleased to read an article in *The Wall Street Journal*[28] about how AstraZeneca established a nine-person team called the Emerging Innovation Unit to give new life to drugs that were previously rejected by the company because they did not work in a certain therapeutic area. The argument was that if the drugs are safe, there could be an opportunity for them to shine in a different area.

Essentially, AstraZeneca is revisiting the cutting-room floor of its R&D labs, an activity that has repeatedly been shown to be valuable in developing breakthroughs. There are many examples

---

28  Denise Roland, "AstraZeneca Gives Rejected Drugs a Second Life," *The Wall Street Journal* (March 13, 2017), https://www.wsj.com/articles/astrazeneca-gives-rejected-drugs-a-second-life-1489402801.

of this practice, known as *drug repositioning*, where compounds that were originally developed for one purpose get redeployed and become market successes in treating another condition. This practice has many benefits, most notably that these drugs have already passed through phase I safety trials and can go directly to stage II efficacy testing. This saves a significant amount of time and money in a process that takes about twelve years to bring a drug from lab to market, with a cost in excess of $2 billion.

The AstraZeneca department, part of an overall R&D revamp strategy, operates on many of the principles of reframing and experiential innovation. First, the company accepts that there may be potential gold in R&D efforts that were previously unfruitful. Then it dedicates resources toward revitalizing them. Additionally, this unit has made collaboration with university researchers a priority. Collaboration and sharing are core pillars of networked improvement and help the company make progress toward achieving its overall goal, which is to dramatically improve its R&D output.

Experiential innovation is all about creating profoundly altering and remarkably enhanced experiences by creatively repackaging existing elements into solutions that are highly valued. Yes, it involves originality, creativity, and new thinking, but the intention is to rethink human experiences rather than focus on the basic and original research that advances science and drives many reframing activities. The AstraZeneca unit discussed previously was not in the business of developing brand-new compounds; it was in the business of using existing developments to create new experiences.

The genius idea for many of the greatest innovations in history was taking existing pieces of functionality and creating unique value. Johannes Gutenberg created his movable-type printing press in the fifteenth century. This invention is often regarded as one of the greatest of all time. Before Gutenberg, the process of printing was laborious and expensive. There were two ways to produce books. The first was dipping woodblocks, which had characters and images chiseled into them, in ink and meticulously pressing them evenly onto paper or cloth. The other option was slowly, carefully, and deliberately writing the manuscript by hand. In today's parlance, neither method was scalable. Writing books was truly a painstaking, time-consuming, and expensive process.

While the idea of a movable-type printing press originated in China (and separately in Korea) centuries before Gutenberg, he is the person credited with this discovery. His genius idea was to combine readily available components into a practical system for printing. He rethought the printing process by using individual components (uppercase and lowercase letters and punctuation marks) instead of blocks, and manipulating the existing parts of a wine press and a coin punch to create a cost-effective way to produce books.

Centuries after the creation of Gutenberg's printing press, the founders of the popular ride-sharing service Uber were successful in connecting existing elements of technology and lifestyle—including personal vehicle ownership, driver availability, smartphone ownership, mobile and GPS technology, and the latent need for riders to have a better customer experience—into a service that helped rocket the company to a $50 billion valuation faster than any other in history.

Experiential innovation is driven by connective creativity. Steve Jobs, widely regarded as one of the greatest innovators of this generation, summarized the concept of connective creativity well by saying, "Creativity is just connecting things. When you ask creative people how they did something, they feel a little guilty because they didn't really *do* it; they just *saw* something. It seemed obvious to them after a while."[29]

## Building an experiential innovation capability

The examples presented in the previous section show that many talented individuals and companies have had the vision and perseverance to develop innovations via the creation of new experiences. However, the question is whether this process can be institutionalized and developed into a core function that can be repeated and measured, or will always remain something that is only achieved by a rare breed of extremely talented and gifted people operating under the right set of circumstances. More specifically, can companies instill a level of discipline, with the right set of methods and tools, to increase the success rate of experiential innovation? Can experiential innovation be done by the rest of us?

Startups excel at experiential innovation. Successful startups have often combined individual pieces of existing functionality into a

---

29   Gary Wolf, "Steve Jobs: The Next Insanely Great Thing," *Wired* (February 1, 1996), https://www.wired.com/1996/02/jobs-2.

valuable, integrated package in a way that radically alters experiences. Because of a powerful desire to emulate these visible startup successes, many corporations in recent years have started building internal startup teams. Only time will tell if these initiatives will be successful; there are far too many differences between real startups and those within corporations to assume they will be successful. Companies may try to bring the startup culture to their organizations, but in reality, the most entrepreneurial people are either becoming founders of or joining real startups. Working at an internal startup unit within Company X still means being employed at Company X.

I do believe that the strength of the corporation, combined with the agility and freedom of thinking like a startup, can be a good approach to developing transformative innovations. But the focus needs to be on experience transformations. This can be done by using *experience journeys*.

## Experience journeys

An experiential innovation begins and ends with an experience journey. The bigger the innovation, the more it changes and enhances a human experience. The experience journey is the process through which people (who may or may not be your customers today) accomplish a task or go through an experience, such as the following:

- Getting on an airplane
- Building a home network
- Treating a medical disorder

- Getting from point A to point B
- Staying close to loved ones
- Shopping for a car
- Doing a load of laundry
- Playing a game
- Negotiating a contract
- Going through any one of the virtually infinite experiences we engage in daily

The goal for experiential innovation is to take a current experience and develop a radical improvement to it. Think of this as a tenfold improvement, not a 10 percent improvement. Henry Ford's assembly line reduced the time to manufacture a car from over twelve hours to under two hours, and his factory went from producing a hundred cars a day to a thousand cars a day. This is an example of the impact we should be looking for, and can bring about, by experiential innovation. This chapter will present a framework for building a disciplined practice of and expertise in experiential innovation.

Three steps are required for experiential innovation:

1. Identify the current experience journey.

2. Develop a new experience journey.

3. Articulate the experience delta.

# Identifying the current experience journey

The first step to institutionalizing experiential innovation is identifying a relevant experience journey that you would like to alter and improve. The experience journey is the description of a desired outcome and the listing of every step within the experience. The experience starts with the first step and ends when the outcome of the journey is achieved. Most great innovators do this process instinctively; they have a keen sense of the experience they are improving.

However, to make this a replicable practice in a corporation, going through the process of listing out the specific steps of the journey is a good place to start. Lay out a step-by-step progression of the current experiences necessary to achieve a specific outcome. As a simplistic example, we can examine the experience journey for washing clothes. Let's say your desired outcome is getting clothes clean and ready to wear. The steps along the journey may include the following:

1. Clothes get dirty

2. Throw clothes in hamper

3. Wait a few days

4. Find time to do laundry

5. Separate clothes

6. Pretreat with stain remover

7. Set the washing machine to the right settings

8. Load machine

9. Add laundry detergent

10. Start machine

11. Wait for 45 minutes

12. Remove lint

13. Put clothes in dryer

14. Add fabric softener

15. Set the drying level

16. Run dryer

17. Wait 30–45 minutes

18. Fold or iron

19. Replace in closet and dresser

20. Wear and get them dirty all over again

Assuming this is the journey you want to alter, you can generate many questions to help identify ways to improve the process. For example, how can the cost of this process be reduced from, say, $1.50 a load to $0.15 a load? How can the time required be shrunk from two hours to fifteen minutes? Or you can come up with even more questions that will lead to transformative innovations: Why do we even need to wash clothes? Why can't we have disposable and biodegradable clothes that reduce the overall cost of ownership of clothing and appeal to diverse fashion senses? Or why doesn't simply tossing clothes in the hamper in my closet result in clean clothes? Some of these questions, at first sight, may seem impractical, but that is the idea. As we have repeatedly seen, just about every great innovation was considered silly by the experts in the field. Developing an accurate list of steps, questioning every assumption, and trying to develop transformational enhancements to the process are the crux of the experience journey.

While the laundry scenario is just an example, the number of experience journeys is virtually infinite. You can pick or create any one, or even part of one, that may be relevant to your business, as long as you are clear about the outcome and the steps along the way. Listing out the steps of an experience journey will involve multiple people collaborating to develop accurate scenarios. The steps needed to achieve a specific outcome may vary for diverse groups of customers or for different geographies or demographics, which is why it is essential to have an accurate and contextual understanding of the scenarios and steps taken within a journey. Without an accurate understanding of the current journey, any improvement efforts are fraught with risks.

## ACCURACY AND CONTEXT

Gillette learned this lesson the hard way while launching a low-price razor blade in India. The company knew that a vast portion of the country, hundreds of millions of lower-income people, still used double-edged T-shaped razors with no protection between the blade and skin. This was a prime opportunity for Gillette to innovate and provide this segment with a low-cost modern razor that would be safer and more effective than the current alternatives. Given the size of the potential market, the opportunity would be enormous if it developed the right product for this set of customers.[30]

Gillette did what many companies do and went through a process to understand the experience journey. In this instance, it wanted to understand the shaving habits of Indian males. It knew that Indian men typically had thicker facial hair and shaved less frequently than Americans, which meant that when they shaved, they were shaving hair that was both denser and longer. The company started with that knowledge and developed a push bar that slid up and down to unclog the razor when it collected hair. This innovation consequently made shaving easier and more effective for Indian facial hair and shaving habits.

As most smart and customer-focused companies would do, Boston-based Gillette invited a group of Indian students from nearby MIT to test their new razor. The product tested well with this group of students, and Gillette decided to introduce it to the market. However, when Gillette launched the new razor in India in 2002, the product was a flop. Company executives were baffled by the product's failure until they traveled to rural India. There, they observed men using the new razors with a cup of water to shave. All of the test subjects in Boston had used running water, which was a requirement for the product to work effectively.

This example demonstrates the need to be accurate and contextual in developing an experience journey. Gillette assumed that the

---

30  Mae Anderson, "How India Helped Gillette Rethink the Razor," *Boston Globe* (October 4, 2013), https://www.bostonglobe.com/business/2013/10/03/cheap -razor-made-after-watches-indians-shave/NSQpOGAotpEfarkNmxIfcK/story. html.

skin and hair type were the key factors driving this innovation, when in fact it missed critical components of the experience journey, such as the fact that its target customers lacked access to running water. Of course, once Gillette had a clearer picture of the experience journey, it was able to build an innovative product at the right price point and grow its market share in India to 49 percent, a significant jump from the 37 percent of a few years earlier.

## ETHNOGRAPHY

One way to develop an accurate experience journey is by using ethnography. *Ethnography* is the observation of people going through experiences in their natural environments. Ethnography is one of the most underutilized tools by organizations and is likely the most valuable approach for understanding the steps of an experience journey. Ethnography is a powerful technique that lets you observe customers in their own settings and identify latent needs and inefficiencies in how things are done. Solving these unstated needs drives innovations.

Done correctly, there is no doubt ethnography can result in experience-enhancing innovations. However, the problems with ethnographic research have included the following:

- It lacks scalability.
- It is too cumbersome, time consuming, and expensive to study experience journeys around the world.
- It is subjective; each viewer may have a different take on what they see.

- It is hard for diverse groups to engage and collaborate while viewing a live customer journey.

Today, with the developments in mobile technology, the ubiquity of video cameras, and the ability for video analytics, ethnographic research is regaining popularity and can be used to drive transformational innovation through the development of effective experience journeys.

## Developing a new experience journey

Once the current experience journey is mapped out in discrete steps, the focus needs to shift to the desired new experience made possible by innovation. How can the experience journey be enhanced? Specifically, which steps of the journey can be improved or made irrelevant? It could involve bypassing all the current steps and getting to the outcome in a new way. The change in the experience—the experience delta—is the result of the innovation.

Experiential innovation needs to be a dedicated function that is staffed by one or more small groups whose sole job is to develop new and transformative experiences. This group needs to be responsible for studying the current experience journeys and developing radically innovative ways of doing things. This is a challenging process, as we are not going to be able to look at every experience and come up with a remarkably enhanced one. However, the following principles can be applied to the process of developing new experiences.

## USING INNOVATION SPARKS

An *innovation spark* is a new idea, approach, or development that is created either within or outside a corporation and may have a specific application within your domain. It could be a new and relevant technology or functionality developed within your own R&D labs, or it could be an industry trend. For example, AI is a broad trend that may have countless valuable applications. AI can be used as an innovation spark, but rather than thinking about the application of AI in general terms within your company, it needs to be applied to specific experience journeys.

## USING FIRST-PRINCIPLES REASONING

Since our goal is to try to improve existing experiences, we need to break each step down to its core and remove any biases or assumptions we may have. First-principles reasoning is an important part of the experiential innovation process. As you develop new experience journeys, it is important to break up all the steps and elements into their first principles. This is done by questioning each step until you get to the core. Then, you figure out new ways to reconnect and recreate each of the first principles to better achieve your outcome.

Using the laundry process example, questioning the need to even wash clothes is first-principles reasoning. Looking at a problem at the foundational level removes current biases and knowledge. If done successfully, you achieve a higher level of abstraction by getting down to a foundational level. And transformational innovation is more likely attainable at a higher level of abstraction.

First-principles reasoning opens your mind to new possibilities because you are no longer focusing on the ways things are currently done. Regardless of what your competitors are doing, what appears to be valuable, or how many customers you think you can get, you are simply taking core foundational facts and using basic and applied knowledge to entertain any and every possibility that can enhance an experience journey.

This type of reasoning can overcome an inherent flaw in humans that prevents the development of new ideas. The theory of *confirmation bias* suggests we have a natural tendency to look for data or facts that support our own preconceived notions. This confirmation bias clouds clear thinking, as we are selectively looking for and internalizing information that supports a conclusion we want. Looking at things the way they are today promotes confirmation bias, but breaking them down into first principles forces us to work from the basic facts and assumptions that are known to be true, thereby reducing biases and foggy thinking.

Improving the current steps in any experience journey leads to advancements and incremental innovation, whereas a reboot or reexamination of the first principles leads to breakthrough and transformational innovation. Building an experiential innovation discipline is not a big investment and is quite likely more effective than other investments in innovation such as the creation and funding of internal startups. This function plays to the strengths of larger organizations and provides a replicable approach that will enhance your chances of developing experience-transforming innovations. Additionally, this function can spur companies to use the reframing activities that are under way within their R&D labs to develop experience-altering offerings.

## Articulating the experience delta

As you'll remember, the experience delta is the difference between a current experience journey and the new or enhanced experience journey. This change between the two experiences becomes the foundation or the vision for an innovation. The experience delta is the currency for defining an innovation, the force behind all activities, and the standard by which to measure the progress of the effort. The larger the experience delta, the greater the societal value provided by the innovation.

For an illustration of an old and new experience journey and the delta between them, let's consider smartphone ride-sharing services such as Uber and Lyft. Before their introduction, the experience of getting from point A to point B (for example, going back to a hotel after dinner at a restaurant) typically involved some of the following steps:

1. Finish dinner and pay the bill.

2. Go outside and look for a taxicab (sometimes in rainy or snowy conditions).

3. Hail cabs as they drive by. Move up and down the street or go to different street corners to improve your results.

4. Repeatedly hail cabs until you finally get one.

5. Communicate your destination to the driver.

6. Settle into the cab; the condition of the cab depends on how lucky you are.

7. Arrive at your destination and pay the cab driver. Calculate and leave an appropriate tip.

8. Exit the cab, perhaps feeling anxious and unsettled by the cab experience.

The new experience with a smartphone ride-share service could be:

1. Pull out your smartphone as you wait for your dinner bill and use the app to summon a car and enter your destination address.

2. Check the app to know exactly where the car is and what time it will arrive.

3. Walk outside as the car comes to your location and go into it.

4. Settle into the car. You expect the car condition to be good and the experience to be pleasant. You know how scores of other passengers have rated this driver.

5. Arrive at your destination.

6. Exit the car knowing that payment is made automatically.

7. Feel safe, since the entire transaction and journey are recorded.

The delta between these two experiences guides the innovation activities. In this example, there are several changed steps that constitute the experience delta:

- You don't go looking for a car; the car comes to you.

- You don't have uncertainty about when you will find a cab; you know exactly, to the minute, when it will arrive. In fact, you can track its progress.

- There is no uncertainty about the condition of the car or the experience of the journey; you expect it to be pleasant.

- You don't need to make a payment. You know the cost, and it is paid directly.

- You have a level of safety, since the entire trip is recorded and you can share your journey with others.

These are just some points that illustrate an experience delta. The goal for any experience delta is to develop such a list.

Ideally, you are trying to maximize the experience delta. The impact of the innovation is proportional to the size of the experience delta (the greater the change between the current and new experience, the bigger the transformation). At this stage in the innovation process it is best to stay focused on the experience delta. If you try to build financial models or estimate market sizes, you are likely to lock yourself into conventional thinking. You simply must believe that if you have a substantial experience delta and are making a positive impact on lives, the market will find a way to reward you for your efforts.

Experience deltas need to measure the impact on people's lives. They may or may not be quantifiable, but they need to demonstrate a marked benefit over the current way of doing something.

# Building the experiential innovation function

As alluded to previously, corporations can improve the rate at which they develop experiential innovations by creating a dedicated experiential innovation discipline that uses experience journeys and deltas to conjure up new and significantly enhanced experiences. The purpose of this function is neither advancement activities (which include listening to customers and recommending improvements in how things are done) nor reframing activities (which are done within R&D settings where science and technology are pushed forward).

Experiential innovation thrives in an inclusive setting with multiple perspectives. Since it involves a combination of domain (core scientific and technical) and applied knowledge, the experiential innovation team should, minimally, include individuals with expertise in those areas. Additionally, the inclusion of other departments (such as operations, product development, or strategic planning) will help create a full cross functional perspective. The key here is to couple domain expertise with other skills. Simply staffing this department with strategists or innovation experts who lack the deep foundational or domain knowledge is not going to be successful.

Developing the experience delta is a four-step process:

1. Develop the long-term goal (create a vision of the new experience and the experience delta).

2. Identify the broad strategies required to achieve the stated experience delta.

3. Identify the intermediate outcomes that allow you to track progress toward your goal.

4.  Identify the specific activities that you will undertake in order to achieve your goal.

It is important to show causal relationships between each step. Additionally, since this is an ongoing improvement initiative, it is critical to have a knowledge repository for the entire process, including documentation of ideas, approaches, and journeys that were attempted or rejected. This knowledge repository is a cornerstone necessary for long-term success in experiential innovation.

Given the unstructured nature of innovation, not every attempt to enhance an experience journey is going to be fruitful. However, since we are implementing innovation activities in a consistent manner, we are in effect employing improvement science. As we go through this process multiple times, we get better at it. This consistent process, each time using knowledge gained from the previous effort, is going to drive experiential innovation.

This means we are learning from our knowledge. Debates and alternative viewpoints are critical in the development of a new experience journey. Knowing what does not work is just as important as knowing what works. This is how knowledge builds and an organization gets better at improving itself.

Every significant innovation has altered human experience, even if that was not the original intention. This chapter has laid out a methodology that starts with the experience journey and leads to the development of an experience delta, the change in experience that serves as the driver and guide for innovation activities. And while not every attempt at developing an experience delta is going to result in a life-changing innovation, you can use this systematic approach as a guide for what you should be looking for in each innovation. The experience delta should become the currency for determining the value of an innovation.

Great discoveries will continue to be made by individual innovators without the formal development of experience journeys and deltas. However, if you are trying to institutionalize the process of innovation or make innovation a consistent competency of an organization, you need a replicable approach that lets you think holistically about how you can enhance experiences. This chapter provided an approach that ties every innovation activity to the change in human experience or the societal value it delivers—the ultimate mark of an innovation.

# CHAPTER 12

# Shared Belief

**The innovation biome, like the natural biome,** requires all elements and ecosystems residing within it to act in concert and support each other. If a corporation seeks to alter its genetic code and transform itself into an innovative juggernaut, then it needs to operate with an exceptionally high degree of conviction that the transition it is embarking upon is going to be successful.

You cannot tiptoe your way into innovation. You simply have to commit to your direction and share your conviction and vision with all related stakeholders, including employees, shareholders, customers, and partners. And everyone around you needs to share in that belief.

Shared belief has incredible power, probably more so than any other factor that drives change. Shared belief in a vision provides everyone involved with the confidence to go all-in and help make the vision a reality. Any ambiguity or second-guessing makes the already challenging task of moving a company in a new direction a lot harder.

In 1965, Gordon Moore, the relatively unknown (at the time) cofounder of Fairchild Semiconductor and Intel Corporation, wrote a paper that included an unbelievable forecast. He wrote (and I'm paraphrasing here) that the number of transistors in an integrated circuit chip would double every year and would continue doing so for the next decade. This prediction (though now slightly revised to doubling every two years) is known as Moore's law.

This wasn't a law that followed the principles of science; rather, it was an observation and prediction that was reasonably true and had the benefit of measurable clarity and a defined time period.

The unique thing about this observation was that although it wasn't a law, it soon became the law. Even though there was really no guarantee that chip capacity would double every two years, everyone shared in the belief, followed it, and expected it to be true, so people started planning for it.

Since people believed computers would become more powerful, they could dream up scenarios and write applications that weren't possible using the current processing power. They could innovate freely because they had confidence that by the time their innovations were released, computer-processing power would have increased sufficiently for users to take advantage of the new capabilities they were developing. Moore's law turned out to be quite accurate and can be credited with the creation and growth of the computer industry as we know it today and with the millions of great innovations that have followed.

This law is actually quite remarkable. Now, at fifty years of age, it has been responsible for the most transformational occurrence of our time: the transition from large bulky computers to the world of information in our pocket. This law of ever-increasing processor capacity continues to lead the way into the future and will be one of the key determinants of whether we will be successful with AI, self-driving cars, and many other breakthroughs that are under development today. To put the impact into perspective, if Moore's law were applied to the auto industry, a 1971 Volkswagen Beetle would travel at three hundred thousand miles per hour and achieve two million miles per gallon at the cost of four cents.[31] The shared belief around Moore's law is largely responsible for driving what is arguably the largest wave of innovation in human history.

Just a few years before Moore's prediction, in 1961, then-president John F. Kennedy made an equally remarkable call to action. He stated, "I believe that this nation should commit itself to achieving the goal, before this decade is out, of landing a man on the moon and returning him safely to the Earth."[32] This was another bold vision for which our society did not have all the necessary elements in hand to realize. But the statement was clear

---

31  "Moore's Law Keeps Going, Defying Expectations," *Scientific American* (May, 2015).

32  John F. Kennedy, "Excerpt from the 'Special Message to the Congress on Urgent National Needs,'" *NASA History* (May 24, 2004), https://www.nasa.gov/vision/space/features/jfk_speech_text.html.

and time bound, and the outcome was measurable. This statement became a shared belief, and everyone involved in the space program played their role in making it a reality. And in 1969 (before the decade was out), one of the most remarkable and boldest visions was realized, once again showing the incredible power of a shared belief. Everyone believed in this statement, and everyone involved worked toward making it happen.

The more you believe in a vision, the more likely you are to help achieve it and, in turn, make the belief real. Belief motivates people to take the necessary actions to make a vision come true, creating an upward cycle.

For the better part of the past decade, most people considered Apple to be the most innovative company in the world. This is not because Apple kept proclaiming it was innovative; it is because it kept churning out one game-changing product after another. Now, everyone expects Apple to produce nothing short of breathtaking innovation. This shared expectation results in exactly that—breakthrough innovations. The perfect upward spiral. The belief is shared by everyone: Apple's customers, employees, shareholders, partners, and even competitors.

A shared belief can coalesce around a vision (such as Moore's law or Kennedy's vision), or it can focus on a culture or way of life for a corporation (such as the creation of an innovation biome). Since an organization has a structure and hierarchy, it is important that the shared belief or the vision be established by the leadership and passed on throughout the company.

The first step to creating an innovation biome is to make it clear, through words and actions, that innovation is a priority. Making innovation a shared belief requires actions that go far beyond appointing an innovation czar or developing an innovation dashboard. It requires thinking about innovation in everything you do. It requires not accepting mediocrity and ensuring that every offering, big or small, enhances a customer experience journey in a meaningful way. This must be an internalized shared belief.

A 2008 survey by McKinsey[33] showed that leadership is the greatest predictor of innovation outcomes. The McKinsey survey studied successful corporate innovations versus those that were unsuccessful. The successful innovations had far greater active participation from company executives compared to the unsuccessful innovations, where executive participation was much lower.

Without leadership commitment, it is impossible to build an innovation biome or an environment where everyone in the organization believes they are creating outstanding offerings. Shared belief starts with leadership, and once the belief is shared, even the largest corporations can pivot adroitly and quickly. As an example, let's look at Microsoft as it was in 1995.

In 1995, although Microsoft wasn't nearly as large as it is today, it was still a formidable company with approximately twenty-thousand employees and revenues approaching $8 billion. The company was riding at the top of a fantastic wave it helped create, often referred to as the PC revolution. As a large and rapidly growing company for which it seemed no obstacle was insurmountable, it could have easily developed tunnel vision and

---

33  Marc de Jon, Nathan Marston, Erik Roth, and Peet van Biljon, "The Eight Essentials of Innovation Performance" (McKinsey & Company, December 2013).

continued pushing along its course. However, for the past year or two there had increasingly been rumblings outside of Microsoft about something that was becoming popular in universities: the Internet. These were the early days of the Internet, and although it had few users, it was growing in popularity. The company began to take notice.

The Microsoft CEO at the time, Bill Gates, sent out a landmark memo asking his executive team to bet the company on the Internet. He labeled it "The Internet Tidal Wave." He shared his prescient view that every PC would soon be connected to the Internet and outlined the risks to Microsoft if it did not fully embrace the new technology. Many companies in Microsoft's position might have done too little or been too late to change, instead continuing happily down their current highly profitable path. Yet Gates saw the risks with the coming change, and in his memo he prescribed a plan for every division of the company to bet on the Internet—not in a small way, but to go all-in. He laid out specific recommendations and actions that each part of the company should do to embrace this new tidal wave.

Almost overnight, Microsoft went from having no Internet capabilities in its products to embracing the Internet in every single thing it did. As we well know today, the Internet did indeed change everything. Microsoft, with the memo written by its CEO, established a shared belief across the company that the entire organization needed to make significant changes and embrace a new way of thinking to stay relevant. And they did. Today, over twenty years later, Microsoft remains one of the most valuable companies in the world.

In many ways, this story is similar to the Kodak story, where

Steven Sasson introduced the digital camera as a new and potentially revolutionary technology to the company. However, the ending could not have been more dissimilar. While Kodak resisted the change as a threat to its profitable business model, Microsoft embraced it and made the advent of the Internet its rallying cry, betting the company on it.

This is the power of a shared belief—the entire organization rallying around a common vision and credo. I know this because I was part of this Microsoft story. I was part of the team that shared in this belief. All of my coworkers did, and we all did our part to help realize this belief. And I saw how a large, industry-leading, complex organization could suddenly act with gazelle-like agility in adopting such a radical change. We were able to do so because turning on a dime is a lot easier when everyone is turning in the same direction.

Successful companies aren't one-hit wonders; they continue making bold bets despite losing some along the way. Today, in 2017, Microsoft is doing it again and going all-in with AI. As Satya Nadella, the current CEO of Microsoft, states, "We are infusing AI into everything we deliver across our computing platforms and experiences."[34] The ending of this story is still to be written, but if history holds true, another shared belief will drive the Microsoft juggernaut to lead the next wave of computing.

If you believe in a vision, you cannot be timid. The way to get

---

34 Microsoft News Center, "Microsoft Expands Artificial Intelligence (AI) Efforts with Creation of New Microsoft AI and Research Group" (September 29, 2016), https://news.microsoft.com/2016/09/29/microsoft-expands-artificial -intelligence-ai-efforts-with-creation-of-new-microsoft-ai-and-research -group/#RA41Wg0O2M3QW5Ge.97.

to a state of shared belief is to live the vision you are sharing. In the Microsoft example, there was nothing half-hearted about the intention to embrace the Internet. With many innovations, companies often don't act boldly or convincingly enough and instead try to tiptoe their way into new areas with the goal of learning as they go. This lack of total commitment often prevents success. So, while the launch-fast, learn-fast, fail-fast philosophy being applied in many companies today has a lot of merits and works better in certain sectors than others, it only works if the offering is given a real chance of success. Otherwise, companies are going to have a lot of failures even as the leaders feel good about themselves, believing they are doing the right thing.

Startups don't have the luxury of selecting what projects to prioritize and work on, or choosing one of several competing business plans in front of them. Nor do they have existing franchises and product lines to worry about in terms of growth or cannibalization. They usually have one idea and can make it work only if they go all-in with everyone sharing the same vision. They make a full and total commitment to their idea and then do the best job they can to execute on it.

If corporations want to learn from and emulate startups in an attempt to become more innovative, then they should adopt this startup mindset—not startup techniques, culture, or freedom, or the cool offices. It is the shared belief and total commitment to a cause that everyone needs to implement, regardless of the size of the organization. This commitment and conviction is going to build a culture of creating repeated breakthroughs.

Microsoft is not the only success story. Other large companies have altered their trajectory by making big, bet-the-company moves. In 2007, Apple was a behemoth in the technology sector with approximately $24 billion in revenues (which is less than a tenth of its revenues today), and it was the highly admired creator of one of the most desired products on the planet, the iPod. That year Apple sold over 50 million iPods and about 2 billion songs on its related endeavor, iTunes.

Conventional wisdom dictates that you just don't go out and risk the sexiest product of the time with an untested device, but that is exactly what Apple did with the introduction of the iPhone that year. Apple went all-in on the iPhone, a product that has not only vaulted Apple to its current status as the most valuable company in the world, but also revolutionized how an entire generation lives.

The launch of the iPhone, during the heyday of the iPod, was a gutsy move by a large corporation. But the risk of not going all-in opens the door for someone else to win over your customers. The example of the iPhone cannibalizing the iPod can be summarized by a common sentiment echoed by then Apple CEO Steve Jobs, who stated, "If you don't cannibalize yourself, someone else will."[35]

Going all-in is neither a new phenomenon nor isolated to technology-sector darlings. Companies throughout history have made big bets in new areas, knowing full well that if they were successful, a large part of their existing business would vanish.

Decades before Apple's big bet on the iPhone, another business leader, William Cooper Procter, the chairman of Procter & Gamble (and grandson of the company's cofounder), made a similar bet in

---

35   Walter Isaacson, *Steve Jobs* (Simon & Schuster).

the 1930s. Procter & Gamble (P&G) at the time was almost exclusively a soap company, though a successful enterprise. (In 1937, P&G revenues were $230 million, or about $4 billion in today's dollars; this is only a fraction of P&G's approximately $70 billion in annual revenues today.) In 1931, P&G engineers, while out on an exploratory visit to Europe, heard some conversation about a potential development that had no commercial value. They heard that a small textile plant that was unable to obtain soap during the First World War used bile from the cattle remains in a nearby slaughterhouse. This bile was synthesized and used as a dyeing agent in the textile industry, but one of its key properties was that it remained unaffected by hard water. However, it was difficult to make and expensive, and it was unsuitable for use within a home, P&G's forte. There was enough interest, though, for the P&G engineers to ship a small quantity of this substance back to the US to play around with.

The problem P&G and other detergent manufacturers were facing at the time was that traditional laundry soaps, which were all made of natural materials, did not work well with hard water, which was prevalent in many regions of the country. These laundry soaps left an unwanted residue on clothes. P&G researchers wanted to use the technology they picked up from Europe to create a synthetic detergent, which they did and sold as Dreft in 1933. Dreft had only modest success because, while it worked in hard water, it did not clean heavily soiled clothes and left them hard and stiff. It was a solution no one was happy with.

However, P&G was certain that synthetic detergents were the way of the future. William Cooper Procter expressed his commitment to the vision and ensured that the shared belief was communicated throughout the organization; he stated that synthetic detergents "may ruin the soap business, but if anybody is going to ruin the soap business it had be better be Procter & Gamble."[36] A bold, firm, and clear statement, it was precisely the type necessary to move a large organization in one common direction.

For almost a decade, the company went through many iterations and experiments to make a synthetic detergent that worked, but it was simply unable to come up with a satisfactory non-soap product. The company finally admitted defeat and shelved the initiative because everyone thought creating a useful synthetic detergent that worked well was simply not possible.

Everyone except one persistent researcher, Dick Byerly, who refused to give up and kept experimenting with different chemical combinations, trying to find the right formula to create the properties P&G was looking for. He did so quietly, without reporting the work he was doing. Like so many innovators, he pushed forward with trial and error and experimentation for a few years. Finally, the breakthrough occurred when he made the decision to inverse the ratio of some of the chemicals he was using, and he arrived at a structure that would clean clothes well without leaving them stiff.

In 1945, Byerly, along with a few others who knew about his work, were ready to demonstrate the invention to the company's president and executives. The P&G leadership soon realized they had a significant innovation on their hands. Even though they had previously given up on this initiative, they decided to go all-in

---

36 American Chemical Society National Historic Chemical Landmarks, "The Development of Tide Synthetic Detergent (July 19, 2017), http://www.acs.org/content/acs/en/education/whatischemistry/landmarks/tidedetergent.html.

again after seeing the invention work. They became determined to launch the new product, which they named Tide, and take it to market as quickly as possible. We can only guess how much time and potential profit was lost while the company (save for one researcher) had temporarily given up on its vision.

The normal course of market entry involved blind testing a new product with customers in a few cities, refining it, and manufacturing it. This process typically took about three years before a product was made commercially available, and P&G had always followed this schedule. But this time P&G moved forward with a level of conviction and commitment not often seen. It realized that when it had something special in its hands, it needed to act in a special manner. It was afraid that running tests for months would get its product in the hands of competitors who would invariably flood the market with their own offerings. So, P&G decided to go full speed ahead and commit $25 million in 1945 (over $300 million in today's dollars) to manufacturing and marketing an untested product. This was a huge bet on an initiative that felt like a breakthrough but had an uncertain outcome. All P&G had was a firm belief that it needed to bring an exceptional product to market as fast as possible, without waiting on protocol.

P&G had thought that Tide would sell well only in the hard water regions of the country, where synthetic detergents were a marked improvement over soap. Instead the product flew off the shelves everywhere and soon became the number one selling detergent—a position it still holds today, some three-quarters of a century later.

The shared belief inside the company was that Tide was a significant innovation, and this caused every other team involved to innovate in any way it could to support the product's success. Tide sparked a wave of innovation across the company: P&G was the first to advertise detergent on TV, offer free samples inside washing machines, and—decades later—offer detergent pods. It was also a pioneer in the development of soap operas.

The Tide story[37] demonstrates the power of conviction and belief. First, the company had a shared belief that synthetic detergents would be the future, and it was willing to cannibalize an existing franchise to support that vision. Then, the individual conviction and belief of a lone researcher kept the vision alive. Finally, the company again developed a shared conviction when it understood it had a potential breakthrough product. In the end, total commitment to a shared belief led to remarkable success.

Large and complex organizations have many moving parts that sometimes work in concert with each other and at other times move in different directions. For an area that is critical to a company's existence, such as innovation, it is important that everybody in the organization move in the same direction. This is what a shared belief leads to. No one in a company owns innovation or the ability to have great ideas. A shared, or collective, belief around innovation clarifies to everyone in an organization that innovation is a priority, and it gives everybody the freedom to be creative and create new forms of value. A shared belief unshackles innovation and provides the confidence needed for great ideas to be presented to the organization and made public.

---

37  American Chemical Society National Historic Chemical Landmarks, "The Development of Tide Synthetic Detergent" (July 19, 2017), http://www.acs. org/content/acs/en/education/whatischemistry/landmarks/tidedetergent.html.

# CHAPTER 13

# Unleashing Creativity

**We revere and admire the great innovators,** the people who have truly changed the world over the course of history. We often think of these people as geniuses or imagine they have some particular trait we can learn or hire for that will lead to unbridled creativity and priceless innovation. We think there's some secret formula to changing the world, and you pick up books like this one hoping to be the only one to read about it.

Well, the truth is, as you've seen throughout this book, there is no single formula for innovation. It takes a lot of work, luck, and disparate events to combine in just the right way—supported by an organization-wide shared belief in innovation and strategic activities for specific innovation goals.

However, you can encourage the cornerstone of innovation:

creativity. A lack of creativity means you can only continue to improve the methods that are in place. This is linear thinking, which is unlikely to help you create transformations. Without creativity, you'll have no new products or experiences to believe in and no new ideas to be potential game changers.

In order to develop a corporation-wide innovation biome and experience-altering innovations, you need an environment where creativity thrives. You can cultivate this biome by understanding and taking advantage of the fundamental characteristics of creativity, which can be learned, implemented, and improved upon. By understanding the factors that drive creative thinking and ensuring the presence of a corporate mindset necessary to encourage creativity, you can let innovation of every type thrive.

## The relationship between intelligence and creativity

Let's tackle the first part of our assumption about great innovators and creators: Are they geniuses? Maybe. But if creating transformational innovations requires that we hire a bunch of Einsteins, we should simply give up now, because it is going to be nearly impossible to find those incredibly rare and gifted minds. However, there are ways to encourage average smart people to create innovations that can be just as transformative.

Let's start by breaking creativity into two pieces to see if we can replicate the output of those brilliant minds. *Creative potential* is an individual's ability to generate something new and novel. *Creative achievement* is their ability to follow through on the creative urge—to implement the innovation. Both are required for innovation; without the idea, you have nothing to implement, and without follow-through, you just have daydreams. The people we consider as great innovators likely have both abilities in spades, but we can create something similar by having multiple people with different abilities work together. This is why a pair of cofounders, each bringing a unique set of skills, can work well together and bring out the best in each other, leading to a successful company—and, in some instances, world-changing innovation.

Just as you have to map the right activity to your targeted-innovation type, it is imperative to match the right set of skills to the desired outcome. For instance, an individual who is a high achiever in an executional capacity (someone with high creative achievement skills) may not be successful if they are placed in a situation that requires creative potential. Pairing this person with someone who has high creative potential, though, may lead to better results. Unleashing creativity requires an understanding of people's strengths, and you must staff innovation initiatives with a group of people whose skills encompass both creative potential and creative achievement.

An interesting study[38] showed a positive correlation between intelligence and creative potential. This means that a person who is more intelligent is likely to be more creative (and vice versa). This may be because creativity is a complex task that draws on the brain processes that are also related to IQ.

However, this correlation vanishes after a threshold (at an

---

38  Emanuel Jauk, Mathias Benedek, Beate Dunst, and Aljoscha C. Neubauer, "The Relationship between Intelligence and Creativity: New Support for the Threshold Hypothesis by Means of Empirical Breakpoint Detection," *Intelligence*, vol. 41 (July–August 2013): 212–221.

approximate IQ level of 120). After that point, how smart the person is has no clear link to their creativity. While an IQ of 120 is certainly high—considered by many experts as the cusp between high-average and superior—it is by no means near the genius-level IQs we often associate with brilliant innovators.

The study also showed that, although intelligence (up to the 120 IQ threshold) relates to creative potential, there is no evidence linking intelligence to creative *achievement*. This means that follow-through is possible across a wide range of intellectual ability and does not relate to intelligence at all.

In a practical setting, this suggests that, although creativity is a complex task, it can be unleashed within the normal range of intellectual prowess found within corporations. Your company likely has all the required elements to achieve any level of transformative innovation you desire, but they must be assembled effectively to cultivate creativity and exist in an environment where creativity is given the best chance of success.

## The components of creativity

Every organization has its own methodology for encouraging creativity, and many of these methods are successful. However, many individual and environmental factors drive creativity. The right creativity attributes are necessary to spur the process forward.

Dr. Teresa Amabile, a long-time expert in creativity research, distilled creativity into the following four components:[39]

---

39  Teresa M. Amabile, *Componential Theory of Creativity* (Harvard Business School, 2012).

- Domain expertise
- Personality traits conducive to creativity
- Intrinsic motivation
- A corporate culture that values creativity

## DOMAIN EXPERTISE

The domain you are attempting innovation in—from social networking to fabric softener—necessarily requires some level of expertise. This is why outsourcing or hiring a consultant or strategist to create your innovation often fails. To arrive at new ideas in a domain requires a core of knowledge about that domain; only a baseline of current knowledge can lead to new knowledge. Most great innovations in science, technology, art, medicine, or any other discipline, are driven by people who have a strong understanding of their domain. If you don't understand your domain, you are not likely to advance it or build the next generation of value.

## PERSONALITY TRAITS CONDUCIVE TO CREATIVITY

Creativity also requires a set of skills—intrinsic in certain people—that drive innovation, such as the following:

- Independence
- Risk taking
- Self-discipline
- A tolerance for ambiguity

- An ability to view different perspectives
- An openness to new experiences
- An ability to synthesize information

These are traits that all innovators have in common. Many people within your company may possess these traits, but they may not be aware they have them and don't consider themselves creative—unless they are put into an environment to create something new. Assessing these skills is essential if you are looking to reproduce and reconstitute the innovation process.

This brings up a common misconception about creativity[40]: that it comes from "creative types." That usually means designers, artists, writers, and so on. However, innovation comes from everywhere. The most creative people tend to be those who have these creativity skills combined with other attributes, such as considerable expertise in the domains in which innovation is happening.

## INTRINSIC MOTIVATION

Intrinsic task motivation is a key component of creativity. *Intrinsic motivation* is the motivation to undertake a task or solve a problem because it is interesting, personally challenging, or satisfying. This contrasts with *extrinsic motivation*, where a task is undertaken for rewards, for evaluation, or as a requirement. As Dr. Amabile

---

40   Bill Breen, "The 6 Myths of Creativity," *Fast Company*, issue 89
     (December 2004), https://www.fastcompany.com/51559/6-myths-creativity.

highlights, people are most creative when they feel motivated primarily by the enjoyment, satisfaction, and challenge of the work itself and their interest in it.

This brings up another misconception[41]: compensation as a motivator of creativity. Money is an extrinsic motivator, and the promise of bonuses and rewards often makes people risk averse, inhibiting innovation.

Extrinsic motivation can undermine intrinsic motivation and should be absent if the desire is to spur creativity and drive innovation. However, eliminating negative extrinsic motivators is often hard to achieve in a corporate environment.

## CORPORATE CULTURE

Your corporate culture—the social environment of your organization—consists of the factors that surround the innovation activity, including intrinsic and extrinsic motivations. There are many organizational barriers preventing creativity, including criticism, organizational politics, and risk aversion.

There are several common misconceptions[42] around corporate culture:

### Time pressure fuels creativity

Having strict deadlines and penalties for failing to create a new product within a certain period is a sure path to failure. People tend to be

---

41  Ibid.
42  Ibid.

least creative under time pressure. Creativity requires an incubation period—time to soak in a problem and let ideas bubble up.

## Fear forces breakthroughs

Creativity is negatively correlated with fear and anxiety. This means that the more fear you instill in your innovation team, the less likely they will be to successfully create something new. You don't grow flowers by threatening them; you give them rich soil, water, and sunlight and get out of the way.

## Competition beats collaboration

The most creative teams are the ones that have the confidence to share and debate ideas, not the ones who compete for recognition and stop sharing information.

## A streamlined organization is a creative organization

Streamlining or downsizing leads to many negative outcomes in your innovation team, such as uncertainty, disengagement, and a lower sense of autonomy. These traits prevent creativity. On the other hand, creativity is enhanced in a positive, collaborative, and diversely skilled environment that offers the freedom to operate independently and the organizational support to be creative and develop new ideas.

As you develop an innovation biome or assemble teams for driving experiential innovation initiatives, understanding and supporting these four components of creativity is likely to provide the highest chance of success.

# Brainstorming doesn't work

Now that we understand the components that enable creativity, we need to extract creative ideas from our teams so we can go out and develop market-leading breakthroughs. For most companies, an all-too-common approach is to find a few inventive people who are perceived to be smart thought leaders and high achievers and assign them to a small group to brainstorm creative ideas and potential breakthroughs. Most innovation initiatives, such as innovation sprints, involve a small group of thinkers like this assigned to develop new and creative solutions.

Although many of us can relate to this approach, it may not always help with innovation. In fact, it may impede the innovation process. The question we need to ask ourselves is how to maximize creative output. Should this be done using group brainstorming, as we have always done, or should we encourage innovation to be managed individually by the right set of people?

## GROUP INNOVATION

The literature and research on the subject does not support the fact that collaborative thinking (brainstorming) is superior to individual thinking in the development of higher-value creative output. Researchers at Yale University[43] compared the productivity of brainstorming groups with individual thinking to determine

---

43   Donald W. Taylor, Paul C. Berry, and Clifford H. Block, "Does Group Participation When Using Brainstorming Facilitate or Inhibit Creative Thinking?" *Administrative Science Quarterly*, vol. 3 (1958): 23–47.

the quantity and quality of creative ideas emanating from each technique. The researchers found that the number of ideas coming from the brainstorming groups was markedly fewer than those developed by individuals, both in terms of the grand total and the unique ideas produced. They concluded that people working individually are more effective at developing creative solutions than when brainstorming in a group, as group participation inhibits creative thinking. There are two primary reasons for this difference: In the brainstorming sessions, strong emphasis was placed on avoiding criticism, and more people tended to follow the same train of thought—what we call *groupthink*.

Since group brainstorming sessions will always be part of corporate life, it is important to understand the flaws that need to be fixed to maximize creative output. First, brainstorming sessions tend to focus on information that group participants have in common instead of bringing out unique expertise. Additionally, some participants are afraid of sharing ideas at the risk of appearing foolish. Others may coast because they don't feel accountable. Some people may have social and cultural barriers preventing them from sharing ideas. Or they may simply be introverts who have great ideas but are unable to share them effectively in a group setting. Sometimes participants can't express their thoughts because others monopolize the conversation. As we have all experienced, many of these brainstorming sessions are often dominated by the highest-paid people or vocal participants who most want to make their presence felt. Certainly, all of these factors create an unwelcome setting that discourages creative thinking.

## HYBRID INNOVATION

Most evidence, however, suggests that the best course of action to enhance creativity appears to be a hybrid model, where individuals are given space to do their own independent thinking, followed by an opportunity to collaborate, share developments, and refine ideas.

As Steven Johnson reports,[44] a study at McGill University followed researchers in four different molecular biology laboratories to understand when and where breakthroughs happen. They found that most of the breakthroughs occurred during meetings where the researchers would informally share and discuss their work. Innovations did not happen when researchers worked solo in their labs; innovation and breakthroughs happened at conference tables. The group interaction helped researchers who worked independently to look at their research in a new light, and the sharing of ideas resulted in the creation of breakthroughs.

Another technique to unleash creativity is *brainwriting*. This technique allows for sharing of written ideas in groups and eliminates many of the flaws of brainstorming. Brainwriting often produces more and better ideas than brainstorming.[45]

Brainwriting takes away some of the negative effects of brainstorming. With this technique, individuals involved in a creative initiative write down their ideas and pass them on to colleagues for refinement or comment. The social and cultural barriers of

---

44  Steven Johnson, *Where Good Ideas Come From: The Natural History of Innovation* (Riverhead Books, 2010).

45  Paul B. Paulus and Huei-Chuan Yang, "Idea Generation in Groups: A Basis for Creativity in Organizations," *Organizational Behavior and Human Decision Processes*, vol. 82 (2000): 76–87.

brainstorming are reduced, and participants feel more empowered to share ideas, resulting in a more innovative set of ideas for
consideration.

## It's all about the right team

Unleashing creativity is a complex function. It is dependent on the
characteristics of people, their expertise in the problem they are
trying to solve, their intelligence, the cultural environment, the
rewards and motivation, and countless other factors (of which only
a few are discussed in this chapter). But creativity can thrive with
the right set of people operating within the right environment. If a
company's goal is to become more innovative through the development of creative solutions, but the right people and circumstances
aren't in place, then no meaningful output can be generated.

Companies often tend to create an internal innovation unit and
staff it with high performers, people who have done well in other
disciplines, younger employees who haven't yet been engulfed by
the system, or workers perceived as independent thinkers. Or they
reward people for doing excellent work on a project by placing
them in an innovation center. This may not result in the outcomes
they are hoping for. Your best bet is to identify domain experts
who exhibit creative traits (including both divergent thinking—
free association of ideas—and convergent thinking, which is more
logical and structured) and are motivated by the task at hand (as
opposed to promotion, status elevation, or other rewards). You
should then provide a positive environment to support their efforts.

# CHAPTER 14

# Diffusion

**Just about every innovation story we have covered** so far has been a new development created through a slow and deliberate process filled with missteps, trial and error, and all the other attributes we have discussed in depth. We have seen examples of inventions that languished for years, and often decades, before they were picked up by a new set of people or under different circumstances, or because of unrelated parallel developments. These inventions became world-changing innovations when they were adopted by millions of people, and they radically added societal value.

For the innovations to augment societal value, society had to first adopt and use them. And despite the trials and tribulations that characterized the development of these innovations, their adoption rates exploded once their value was seen by their users, and there was no turning back. Societal value is hard to hide, and broad adoption of valuable innovations has always been rapid and seems to be getting faster with each innovation.

Consider two recent innovations that continue to alter the lives of billions of people today: smartphones and Facebook. It has taken just a decade for smartphone ownership to grow from virtually zero to over 50 percent of the adult population in developed countries, and for the number of Facebook users to grow from almost nothing to over a billion daily active users.

While these levels of growth for great innovations may seem to be a characteristic of the Internet age, this is not a new phenomenon. The first telegraphic message was sent in 1844, and within a decade more than 20,000 miles of telegraph lines crisscrossed the US. By 1858, telegraph cable was successfully laid across the Atlantic Ocean, extending for over 2,000 miles, sometimes at a depth of more than 2 miles.[46] This remarkable achievement reduced the time required for information to flow between North America and Europe from a matter of weeks (the time it took for ships to cross the Atlantic) to just a couple of minutes through the freshly laid telegraph wire. While this adoption rate might not seem rapid today, this would have been considered a warp-speed development (to use current jargon) in the mid-1800s. Of course, as history would have it, telegraph use began slowly, rapidly caught on, disrupted the world, slowed down, and

---

46  History.com, "1858: First Transatlantic Telegraph Cable Completed," History. com website, http://www.history.com/this-day-in-history/first-transatlantic -telegraph-cable-completed.

eventually (like every other innovation) was replaced by newer and better technologies. The adoption of the telegraph followed the fundamental principle of diffusion that applies to every single innovation.

## The diffusion S-curve

The diffusion of innovations is one of the most researched and well-established principles in social science. Diffusion is the process by which an innovation is communicated through certain channels over time among the members of a social system.[47] The diffusion-of-innovation model is represented by the familiar S-curve, where adoption of a new idea is slow at first because it is accepted only by Innovators and Early Adopters. The rate of acceptance of the innovation then increases swiftly as it is adopted by the Early and Late Majority. The pace of acceptance slows down again as the laggards adopt it, at which point it is no longer new.

The following image demonstrates Rogers's popular diffusion curve showing an innovation's progress over time and the phases it goes through before it reaches all of its intended users. The bell curve represents the progressive groups of adopters, and the S-curve highlights the path an innovation takes until it attains its maximum potential market share.

---

47   Everett M. Rogers, *Diffusion of Innovations* (Free Press, 2003).

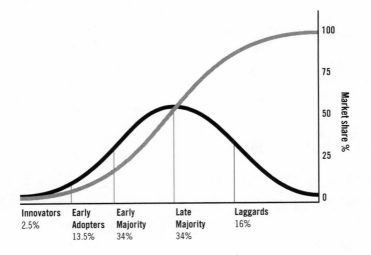

| Innovators | Early Adopters | Early Majority | Late Majority | Laggards |
|---|---|---|---|---|
| 2.5% | 13.5% | 34% | 34% | 16% |

The diffusion model suggests that new developments are first adopted by a small group of people labeled the Innovators, who are bold and unafraid to take a risk by being the first to try something new. Some of these people may have the highest desire and motivation to use the innovation (as in the case of a new cancer treatment that lacks good evidence of efficacy and safety but for which there is no appropriate alternative). Or they may be people who have been influential in the development of the innovation. Innovators are a small set of people, usually 2.5 percent of the total users. (The 2.5 percent comes from being two standard deviations below the mean. The mean is the point where 50 percent of potential users have adopted the innovation.)

The next set, or another 13.5 percent of adopters, are the Early Adopters. These are opinion leaders or influencers in their field whose judgments play a key role in the adoption of the innovation. Others look to them for guidance. This is the group of people that sets the tone for how rapidly an innovation will spread within a community. (The 13.5 percent is the difference between one and two standard deviations below the mean.)

The Early Majority constitutes about 34 percent of the adopters. These individuals are the cautious, careful, and diligent users who do their research before adopting something new. This is an important group, as they are the group of users who make an innovation mainstream. The Early Majority requires education and encouragement, as their decision process is deliberate and analytical. The earlier success of the innovation and the positive reinforcement from the Early Adopters drive their adoption. (The 34 percent represents one standard deviation below the mean.)

Once the innovation reaches 50 percent of its likely number of users, the Late Majority starts adopting it. The Late Majority, about a third of the total potential users (one standard deviation above the mean), are slow to adopt an innovation for many reasons, including perceived need and economic motivation.

The final 16 percent (two standard deviations above the mean) of adopters, Laggards, are at the tail end of the diffusion curve. The rate of growth of users is the slowest here, and users need to be absolutely convinced that the benefits of the innovation significantly outweigh the costs (financial or other, such as the time involved in learning something new).

The diffusion model has withstood the test of time. Just about every innovation in the past hundred years has followed the diffusion S-curve. Interestingly, as we progress through the century, we notice the diffusion cycle getting increasingly steeper, implying that the rates of adoption are getting faster and faster all the time.

For instance, older innovations such as the telephone took over 40 years to reach 50 percent of US households, whereas more recent innovations such as the Internet took under 10 years to get to the same penetration level.

While diffusion happens after an innovation is released, its theory provides some useful clues as to how innovations that are being developed can become successful. Remember, an innovation is nothing if it does not add societal value. And to add societal value, it needs to be adopted and used. While the development of an innovation itself is unpredictable, its diffusion is smooth and predictable.

## The five drivers of diffusion

According to the majority of approximately seventy-five research studies in the field of diffusion research, five attributes drive the successful adoption of an innovation: relative advantage, compatibility, complexity, trialability, and observability. Everett Rogers's[48] summaries of these five drivers are provided in the following sections.

### RELATIVE ADVANTAGE

Relative advantage is the degree to which an innovation is perceived as better than the idea it replaces. Using the terminology introduced earlier in this book, the concept of relative advantage is similar to the experience delta. The few minutes it took to send a message

---

48    Everett M. Rogers, *Diffusion of Innovations* (Free Press, 2003, 5th ed.).

across the Atlantic Ocean was a huge improvement over the weeks it took prior to the telegraph's introduction. With such a huge relative advantage (or experience delta), it is no surprise that this innovation has gone down as one of the most remarkable in history.

## COMPATIBILITY

Compatibility is the degree to which an innovation is perceived as consistent with existing values, past experiences, and the needs of potential adopters. Airline frequent-flyer miles was a program perfectly compatible with every other experience of air travel, leading it to become one of the most ubiquitous innovations in the travel industry.

## COMPLEXITY

Complexity is the degree to which an innovation is perceived as relatively difficult to understand and use. The complexity of an innovation is the only attribute inversely proportional to its rate of adoption; that is, the more complex an innovation, the less likely it is to get adopted quickly. While the iPhone was successful for many reasons, particularly due to its high relative advantage over alternatives, its success would not have been as pronounced had it been a device that was complicated to use. The intuitive and easy-to-use interface played a crucial role in its success.

## TRIALABILITY

Trialability is the degree to which an innovation may be experimented with on a limited basis. Every website has a high degree of trialability. There is no cost (monetary or other) associated with visiting a new site, and people are free to visit and make their own judgments on a website's value. Most companies, to spur adoption, routinely use a range of techniques to encourage trialability of innovations.

## OBSERVABILITY

Observability is the degree to which the results of an innovation are visible to others. When the automobile was introduced, its benefits were clearly observable to society, and people not using it could easily see what they were missing.

## THE RELATIVE IMPORTANCE OF EACH DRIVER

These are the five factors to consider when launching an innovation. If your innovation scores high on relative advantage and compatibility and low on complexity, and if you can provide easy trialability and observability, you likely have a winner. Then the focus needs to shift to informing users of these benefits.

These five drivers are not equally weighted. Relative advantage (or the delta between the current experience and the new one resulting from an innovation) is the overwhelmingly important attribute. Relative advantage trumps everything else, and it is important to understand that. For instance, many important innovations have increased complexity, but the experience delta they offer is so large that this increase becomes irrelevant. For example, when automobiles were first introduced, driving a car was a complex undertaking, with recurrent breakdowns, unsuitable roads, lack of fuel availability, and flat tires being a near-daily occurrence—not to mention the learning curve required to understand how to drive it.

However, the delta between the experience of traveling by car versus walking or riding a horse is so huge that it more than surpassed the complex drawbacks. Most new undertakings require new learning. Companies are sometimes caught in a trap where they are hesitant to let an innovation negatively affect ease of use. Yes, if the benefits of the innovation are marginal, then ease of use is a significant issue. But the greater the benefits of the innovation, the less weight the other attributes have in its overall success.

Revisiting the Kodak story one more time, the original digital camera developed by Sasson had a high degree of complexity and poor compatibility with the existing mode of taking and sharing photos, as well as poor trialability and observability. An electronic camera was such a novel concept that it simply did not fit any known mold of photography. The lack of visible benefits was also a factor in suppressing this innovation. However, had the company been able to articulate the experience delta (the possibilities that this new digital technology could bring to photography), it may have realized that the high relative advantage more than compensated for the shortcomings in complexity and compatibility.

## Combining experience with advantage

In today's age of widely available information, any word of a significant gain in an experience journey is going to spread quickly, and innovations with high relative advantages will get adopted rapidly. But in fact, this has been true way before the advent of the Internet and social media. Going back to the 1450s, the founder of the modern printing press, Johannes Gutenberg, tried to keep his invention a secret (presumably because there was no patent protection at this time). However, the experience delta between the old way of producing books and Gutenberg's method was so large and overwhelming that it just could not stay a secret for long. In the next few decades, over twenty-five hundred European cities had acquired printing presses, thereby making the process of printing books mainstream and exhibiting once again the classic diffusion model at work.

## Facing uncertainty

Every innovation has uncertain benefits, and the larger the uncertainty, the slower the adoption of the innovation. Almost all inventors get taken by surprise as their innovations gain popularity by being used in ways they never expected. Consequently, even if an innovation's benefits are uncertain, it sometimes makes sense to release it, since customers may find value or uses that are unintended or unknown to the producer. How the earliest users, the 2.5 percent defined as Innovators, use a product provides invaluable clues to what the innovation can become.

Many new offerings in their early incarnations don't live up to expectations, and this slows down the diffusion process.

Consequently, it is essential that the early incarnations be given a sufficient chance at success. There is much written about launching a minimally viable product, or a product that has just enough functionality for a small group of customers, with the goal of learning from their usage and improving the product quickly. This tactic may work well for startups, but it may be risky for larger corporations. Customers have a certain set of expectations, and a just-enough product may break the trust they have with a brand. Large companies would be advised to find a sample of the earliest users, give them the product as part of a monitored trial, and work with them to co-create an exciting innovation with large societal value.

## Clustering value

Depending on the innovation, it is advisable to develop a cluster of value surrounding it. As discussed in depth in chapter 8, an innovation is often a cluster of offerings that compose an entire ecosystem of value. Whether it was the cluster of value built by Birdseye around frozen foods, or the cluster of value built by Edison around lightbulbs, innovation must be thought of as a comprehensive set of related offerings. While the telegraph was a great invention developed by Samuel Morse, its cluster of value was established when Western Union laid wires across the country to standardize its use. Henry Ford's assembly line innovation involved a cluster of value that included the manufacture of standardized parts that could be used interchangeably, and worker specialization, where unskilled employees could be trained to do just one task and not be holistic and skilled artisans.

While the cluster of value varies for different sectors, it includes developing complementary products and services; enhancing the ability for trial; and providing education, sufficient training, or case references related to the innovation's functionality to accelerate the adoption curve. In essence, building the cluster of value supports the innovation. The cluster of value should be focused on optimizing for the five diffusion attributes discussed in this chapter. Only then are you giving your innovation the best chance of success.

In fact, the three buckets of costs for getting an innovation into the hands of customers are (1) the cost of developing the innovation (typically R&D costs), (2) the cost of informing users about the innovation (typically sales and marketing costs), and (3) the innovation cluster costs (the costs for ensuring the right supporting infrastructure and framework is developed to help the innovation achieve rapid adoption).

For corporations developing offerings with innovative value, it is not simply enough to think about the invention and its marketing and sales. When the innovation is introduced, it is going to follow the standard diffusion curve; the only unknowns are the rate and speed of adoption, which will determine its eventual success (or failure). The principles of diffusion offer a holistic model or framework that needs to be utilized to make an innovation successful.

# PART 4

---

# NURTURING THE INNOVATION BIOME

**The preceding chapters discussed the creation and diffusion** of an innovation. We covered the attributes of innovation and discussed a framework for implementing an innovation biome in your organization. We learned how an innovation does not stop with the creation of the offering and how it can be adopted by users to enhance societal value.

We have discussed most of the components required to build an innovation biome. If you stay true to the principles laid out in this book, your innovation efforts are far more likely than traditional methods to result in the creation of fantastic developments that are loved by your customers.

But it does not end there. You need a way to spread your innovation to the world and track your progress, and the biome needs to be maintained. You need to have a mechanism for staffing and rewarding innovation. And you need to understand how to deal with the ambiguity inherent in innovation and what lessons you can learn when things don't go quite as well as you would like. The final section of the book provides practical considerations for the measurement and management of innovation activities.

# CHAPTER 15

# Measuring Innovation

**Innovation involves a complex set of activities,** and the outcome of innovation activities may not always be linked to specific and measurable inputs. Innovation is a hard concept to measure in a meaningful way. If companies want to rekindle the innovative spirit they were founded on and develop innovation into a core competency, clear metrics are required.

Additionally, if the goal is to make innovation a replicable and consistent activity, then it is important for companies to understand how to get better at improving themselves. Therefore, it is essential to understand the specific activities that yield meaningful outcomes. In other words, a causal relationship model is required between activity and outcome. This is an especially tall order given that innovation is the outcome of many inputs, including activities, culture, people, environment, timing, and knowledge flow, as well as the interconnections between them.

Unfortunately, there are few helpful innovation metrics in place today. Countless metrics for innovation are in use, but many are irrelevant and self-serving, and some may actually prevent innovation. Current innovation metrics generally fall into three buckets: input metrics, process metrics, and output metrics.

Input metrics measure the activities and inputs, such as R&D expenditure and head count, the number of ideas submitted, and the number of innovation projects being worked on, among other factors. Then there are process metrics, which track how innovation is progressing and often include stage-gate metrics measuring idea flow and number of projects funded and piloted. Finally, output metrics include measures such as P&L impact of innovation, number of patents filed, and revenues from new products.

Innovation scorecards and complex dashboards exist at many companies. However, corporations need to be careful about how they measure innovation, since metrics determine activities. For example, if "number of patents filed" is a metric to show how innovative a company is, then the attention goes there, which can take away from efforts to bring the most inspiring products to customers. This focus may result in a lot of effort to get ideas and developments patented and not enough effort to bring great new products to market and create long-lasting customer value. As we have seen, the majority of experiential innovations, rather than new inventions, create massive transformational value from simply connecting dots. Certainly, an increase in the number of patents filed is a good thing and has many positive outcomes, including potentially leading to more innovations, but it is not a measure of whether innovation that builds societal value is happening within an organization.

Another example is the percent of revenues spent in R&D, a common metric used to gauge how innovative an organization is. Yes, R&D expenditure is critical for innovation. Without R&D, it is unlikely that a company will be innovative. But this simply measures how much a company spends and not what it gets in return. And since this metric is tracked and reported, it motivates the company to spend more, not necessarily a healthy thing to do. Companies focus on input metrics because they are tangible and measurable and provide the businesses with confidence (often false) that they are heading in the right direction.

It is also important to note that transformative innovation, the grand new creations that every company thirsts for, takes a long time—often years—and usually requires a bumpy process of trial and error, learning, and experimenting. Traditional innovation metrics are unable to track these activities effectively. One reason is that rewards for metrics achievement are often on a shorter term (usually an annual cycle), so the longer-term activities do not get the right level of attention. Worse yet, there is an inherent motivation (i.e. greater rewards) for managers to focus on initiatives that provide short-term gains, since the outcomes are not guaranteed in longer-term initiatives.

Because the innovation process is so diverse, nebulous, and intangible, the challenge with measuring it is that too many metrics are used and way too much time is spent in the creation of complex dashboards. Many innovation experts list dozens of metrics that organizations should track on a regular basis. This is simply too hard and, in fact, counterproductive, since having a multitude of metrics takes the focus away from the core reasons why companies need to innovate.

Rather than simply putting a lot of different metrics in place, corporations need to develop a framework to understand and measure innovation. As a first step, companies need to understand that innovation measurement is not static—it evolves as the understanding of new-value creation grows and evidence shows which activities work and which do not. Companies also need to realize that innovation is a collaborative activity with many disparate elements that are most productive under the right environment. Consequently, there must be a qualitative measure to understand and evaluate innovation. Companies also need to internalize the fact that data collection to track the success of innovation activities is imprecise, and innovation cannot be measured and managed simply by a set of numbers that certain people are accountable to achieve. Finally, it is critical to be transparent in sharing the progress of innovation efforts and results broadly across the organization.

Innovation metrics simply need to track two primary elements:

1. Progress: Is there progress toward becoming an organization that is increasingly innovative (or, as we define it, is the organization moving closer to developing an innovation biome)? Are the building blocks and culture in place to support and drive growth through innovation?

2. Outcome: Are the activities that are in place yielding desirable results that further the mission of the company?

For innovation activities to be successful, it is important to have a methodology to manage and evaluate the two primary elements. Doing so will lead to the desired set of activities, which in turn are most likely to lead to the desired set of outcomes.

## Progress toward an innovation biome

The first measure—whether a company is building an environment or a biome conducive for innovation—is, by and large, a qualitative one. Though some components can be quantified, the qualitative nature of this measure is something that company executives need to be aware of and assess on an ongoing basis. These components are the essential attributes and activities that drive an ongoing culture of innovation, and reducing them to a few numbers does them a disservice. I understand the sentiments of many executives who believe that everything that needs to be managed must be measured quantitatively. However, the ability to innovate consistently is an evolving and subjective effort that requires an honest discussion to understand progress and its drivers. The process of innovation is about not only getting better at new value creation but also getting better at getting better—in other words, getting better at the innovation process.

There are three areas to focus on here:

## INNOVATION ACTIVITY MAPPING

Innovation activity mapping involves building and reviewing Activity Maps to illustrate how much time, effort, and energy are going toward advancement, reframing, and experiential activities and to evaluate whether the right sets of tools are in place for each set of activities. As we have discussed extensively, different approaches and tools result in distinct kinds of innovation. If the tools and activities are mismatched, there is going to be no forward progress, despite a lot of wheel-spinning effort. The innovation activities need to be mapped, reviewed, understood, and matched with the right set of tools. Building an innovation biome starts with having a clear understanding of whether the innovation activities in progress are equipped for success.

## INNOVATION MINDSET

The innovation mindset addresses whether the people in an organization believe they are in a continual improvement mode, and whether innovation is a priority that is supported and encouraged by the company's leadership. Are the right frameworks in place, and are they broadly known and consistently implemented? Is there a collaborative environment and a system of knowledge sharing across teams? Do employees believe they are empowered to innovate and improve upon the status quo? Employee polls, which are common in most organizations, can track whether an organization has the innovation mindset and employees feel empowered to innovate.

## KNOWLEDGE TO INNOVATE

Do those people responsible for driving improvement and innovation have the basic knowledge of innovation drivers—the attributes that promote and inhibit innovation? Do employees understand the importance of collaborating and being persistent and the risks associated with criticizing new ideas, or chasing the next new shiny object? Does the organization possess the tools required for innovation, and is there a shared-knowledge repository for employees to tap into and build on? Finally, how do people in the organization learn from innovation activities, and how have experiences (successful or otherwise) translated into organizational knowledge that can be applied to future activities?

# Innovation outcomes

Three key measures are used to track the second element (the outcomes of innovation activities) and are discussed in this section. The following three measures are all outcome focused and directly linked to the core purpose of innovation, which is building and sharing inspirational offerings that customers love. And needless to say, success here results in nonlinear growth of revenues, profits, and shareholder value.

## INSPIRATION INDEX

The Inspiration Index measures the rate of customer growth over time. If the customer growth trajectory is high, you have inspired them. It measures the speed with which they embrace new offerings.

The Inspiration Index is used for anything that is new, including enhancements to current offerings (incremental innovation) or the development of business-model-altering offerings (breakthrough or transformational innovation).

The Inspiration Index measures whether a company is developing products that inspire. The products and services in this measure don't have to be new to the market. They simply have to be new to the company. They could include the company's entry into an established or new market, or simply an extension of an existing offering. The company just needs to be able to define something new it has created and track customer growth and sentiments around the innovation.

The Inspiration Index does not measure financial growth, since the only goal here is to measure customer inspiration. Financial rewards may come with customer growth, or they may come later. If you build products and services that inspire, there is little doubt that financial rewards will follow. It took Amazon until 2004, ten years after its founding and seven years after becoming a public company, to record its first profitable year; however, during that decade, there is no doubt that the company was building inspirational offerings that customers loved. Amazon is hardly alone; many of the companies we admire today, including Facebook and Tesla, have spent years building inspiring innovations, knowing that profits will follow.

## VITALITY INDEX

The Vitality Index measures the percentage of current year revenues derived from products and offerings developed in the past X years (usually three to five years).

This is an established metric that is used frequently in companies and has stood the test of time. It was initially developed in 1988 at 3M as an overall measure of innovativeness. This is a valuable metric for companies that want to be in a state of ongoing innovation. The actual targets may vary for different companies. For example, in sectors where new-product introduction is the norm, say, technology or consumer electronics, the Vitality Index may be measured for products introduced in the past eighteen months or two years. In other industries where the rate of product introduction is slower, the Vitality Index may be measured over three or even five years. However, the concept remains unchanged and is true for all companies.

At some point, corporations need to reap rewards from innovative activities. If there is no goal for business growth from innovation, then innovation is not likely to be a priority. Most companies already track this metric as some form of new product sales, but making it an index provides a measurable way to track how innovative a company is on an ongoing basis. When combined, the Vitality Index and the Inspiration Index create a well-rounded picture of the effects of all innovative activities a company engages in.

## TRANSFORMATION INDEX

The Transformation Index measures the number of first-to-market products or services launched, irrespective of success or failure.

If companies want to create industry transformations and disruptions, they must create new categories and enter brand-new spaces. Some of these ventures may be successful and some may not, but this metric is important if a company wants to have an innovation-driven culture where new thinking and bold bets are encouraged.

This is not a volume metric; at most, a corporation or division may have one transformative new bet every year or two. But this metric is important because it drives the right set of activities that create value that has never been seen before, which is needed for success.

This metric promotes experiential innovation through the development of new experiences. These transformations are only possible in a culture where free thinking is encouraged, new ideas are given serious consideration, risk taking is encouraged, and failure is considered okay. Learning how to navigate the idea-to-market process is invaluable.

Even if a company has a single transformative success story once every ten years, the returns are simply phenomenal. But companies need to start somewhere, and establishing and holding themselves accountable to a Transformation Index is a good first step.

\* \* \*

There is no perfect or even right set of metrics. The set presented in the previous section is a rational and relevant list of things to track to determine whether a company's innovation activities are paying off as tangible business results and whether the organization is improving its innovation process. Even if the actual metrics used are different, tracking these two elements effectively is key to monitoring a company's innovation progress. Everything else is noise.

An organization needs to adhere to a set of measures and qualitative discussions that help develop the right set of activities to enhance the rate of innovation. If these activities are implemented uniformly and the results are shared broadly and transparently, then the company is on its way to creating a fruitful and productive innovation biome. This, in turn, will increase its chances for creating offerings that customers embrace and for earning the rewards that go with being at the forefront of innovation.

As with any measurement, you need to track what you want to achieve—in this case, the metrics that lead to the creation of value. It would be wise to focus only on the metrics that lead you to your goals and forget about marginal ones that may look good on a dashboard or press release, but fail to drive your desired outcomes.

# CHAPTER 16

# Maintaining the Innovation Biome

**The outcomes an organization achieves, whether financial or** otherwise, are merely the sum total of the efforts expended by it. Organizations are knowingly or unknowingly wired to get exactly the outcomes they achieve. If they are not innovating or have been seeing flat growth each year, it is simply because of their actions (or inaction). The right set of actions can help a corporation create and sustain an innovation biome where large and small innovations are generated all the time. As a result, the organization will see a set of breakthroughs that propel it skyward, like the grand kapok tree soaring high over the entire landscape.

As we have seen throughout this book, there is no quick fix or single solution that is going to get you onto a journey to innovation greatness. Betting on a single methodology for innovation is a fool's errand with no hope of success. Building and sustaining an innovation biome should be simple, as its concepts are straightforward and can be easily explained in a clear and lucid manner to large organizations. You must follow principles that make logical sense, so an entire organization can understand and implement them. You must implement practices that have endured the test of time—not years or even decades, but centuries and millennia.

However, implementing these simple concepts is not easy and requires ongoing commitment and attention. But if innovation is truly a priority, then the right steps must be followed.

Everything in this book is about creating the innovation biome. It is about getting better so real progress can be made. I have attempted to share evidence-based knowledge about the elements that create and sustain innovation, drawing upon some of the fantastic empirical research done over the last half century on innovation science, creativity science, and other related fields.

The steps to build and maintain an innovation biome are as follows:

## STEP 1

The first step to creating an innovation biome is having the commitment of the organization's leadership and sharing the vision that innovation is the essential activity that will allow the company to sustain relevance in an ever-changing marketplace. Visible and personal commitment, through words and actions, by the leadership is the only way the rest of the organization will internalize the fact that innovation is a priority.

This commitment results in a shared belief where every person within an organization believes they can play a role in innovation and must push the boundaries in every activity. The error of omission (not having everyone play a role) is far greater than the error of commission (playing a role and doing the wrong things). The innovative power of an entire organization is far greater than that of a select few. It will take time and effort to get there, but people want to be innovative and do outstanding work. Once this happens, you will have an unstoppable force.

## STEP 2

Get rid of misconceptions and fallacies that haunt an organization. You will not be successful chasing the next big thing. This is simply because the next big thing is not sitting out there waiting to be plucked. The big breakthrough idea you are looking for is already out there; you just need to pick it up and build unmatched value with it. Innovation is not about the value in creating ideas; it is about the ideas creating value.

## STEP 3

To create an innovation culture, you need to understand its foundational components, the first principles, and then ensure they are present. Without the presence of these components, innovation is highly unlikely, no matter what else you do. The five innovation components we discussed in this book are priming, acceptance, networked development, clustering value, and an environment to catalyze innovation.

## STEP 4

There are different types of innovation activities, including those designed for creating incremental innovation, breakthrough innovation, and transformational innovation. Each of these types of innovation is just as valuable as the other. There is a common misconception that incremental innovation is less desirable, but that is simply not true. Incremental innovation is the essence of an organization; without a culture of continual improvement, big breakthroughs are unlikely to occur. Understand that each of these activities requires different tool sets and approaches. Matching the tools to activities is essential, or else innovation efforts will be for naught.

## STEP 5

Innovation is about altering experiences. The difference between an individual's current experience and the new experience developed through an innovation is the experience delta. The bigger the experience delta, the more impact the innovation will have. Systematic innovation development requires the articulation of the experience delta, which becomes the vision and driving force behind the innovation effort. As organizations get in the habit of creating experience deltas, the process of innovation will become more habitual and eventually be institutionalized.

## STEP 6

Ensure that every dedicated innovation initiative is staffed by people with the right skill set. Simply assigning high achievers or people showing high potential to innovation activities can backfire. Innovation is most likely to happen with people who have expertise in their domain, a set of relevant creativity traits, and the right level and type of motivation, and it requires an environment conducive to creativity. For any dedicated innovation activity, the team must be selected solely based on the ability to create new value.

## STEP 7

Innovations are most likely to have market success if they exhibit a clear advantage over existing experiences. Additionally, an innovation needs to resolve a real need (stated or latent) of customers, have an evident advantage so users can see its benefits, and provide as smooth a path to adoption as possible. Getting an innovation to be successful and widely adopted requires a dedicated focus on these attributes.

## STEP 8

Finally, the right metrics need to be in place to track progress on your innovation strategy. There is no need for complex dashboards tracking a myriad of activities that may or may not result in innovation. The innovation metrics need to be simple, transparent, and something the company can track. The leadership of the organization needs to own the responsibility to deliver on them.

In the preceding chapters, we discussed in detail these points and many techniques your organization can use to maintain an innovation biome. However, a few additional considerations need to be addressed for you to fully develop and maintain a fertile environment that supports and encourages new-value creation.

## Insourcing innovation

An organization's innovation strategy must be insourced. Innovation is a critical foundation of a company's strategy; for it to become an essential activity that is part of the very fabric of an organization, it cannot be outsourced to a consultant, a software platform, a startup incubator, or even an acquisition-led strategy. The capability and expertise to innovate must be developed and nurtured internally. When you think about the most innovative companies in the world, you think of those that are intrinsically innovative, not the ones continually looking externally for guidance during the innovation process. How many great innovations can you think of that came from external guidance? I can't think of too many.

Many executives of large corporations often believe that their organization is slow, rigid, and incapable of nimbly creating breakthroughs. Consequently, they invest in creating startups or innovation incubators within the organization with the hope that these new teams will operate at the level of speed, agility, imagination, and creativity necessary to catalyze the innovation process. These incubators may develop new value; however, there are some risks with this approach, the primary one being that it does not create a culture of innovation across the corporation.

The innovation biome promotes using the full strength and power of the entire corporation to innovate. Building internal or external incubators or startups as an innovation strategy only creates pockets of new-value creation and neutralizes the strengths of the parent organization. It promotes the thinking that innovation is the sole responsibility of the incubator. These investments also have no guarantee of success. If regular startups have a failure rate approaching 80–90 percent, I would imagine the failure rate of corporate-incubated startups would be higher because, while they are designed to act as startups, they do not operate under the same conditions and are really an extension of the mother ship.

Some executives believe they can build an innovation strategy centered on acquisitions. They believe they can let venture capital–funded companies take the risks and, once something promising is developed, simply write a big check and acquire the hot enterprise. While acquisitions that further your mission make perfect sense, pursing acquisitions as an innovation strategy is risky. Shareholders aren't investing in you to act like a venture fund that overpays for acquisitions; they are investing in you to extend and grow your business. Plus, an acquisition-driven strategy for innovation assumes that the core business is going to continue generating the cash needed to make the acquisitions and to cover the years a company has to wait before the acquisition is materially accretive to the company.

The leadership challenge for creating an innovation biome is understanding and internalizing the fact that, like the natural biome, innovation requires a lot of things to happen unceasingly. But when they do happen, even the largest organizations can become innovation powerhouses. Size and resources can be used to strengthen innovation instead of being perceived as an impediment. The simple irony is that large corporations envy the agility of startups and their ability to innovate, and startups envy the resources large companies have to solve any problem they face. Your best bet is to be the best version of you and not try to become someone you are not.

There is rarely a big bang or sudden forceful change for innovation. When someone develops that rare, landscape-altering, supremely desirable, and exceedingly profitable innovation, it may have a big-bang appearance that everyone wants to emulate. But, in reality, it is the culmination of innumerable small activities in place for a long time within a supportive environment. If this is what an organization's leadership aspires to achieve—to go down in history as one of the great creators that changed the world— then its best bet is to develop the right biome that makes it innovative by playing to its strengths.

No matter how large or small your organization is, everybody can develop an innovation biome. The average Fortune 500 company has about fifty-thousand employees. The goal should be to get most of these people committed to a mission around improvement and innovation. Even if they are not directly involved in innovative activities, they need to lend their support to those who are. Innovation should not be limited to a group of five hundred or a thousand people who are dedicated to innovation initiatives or R&D. It is only when everyone in an organization understands that innovation belongs to every single one of them that the full power of the innovation biome can be unleashed.

## Staffing and rewards

Staffing is a critical element that can make or break the creation of an innovation biome. Typically, in a large corporation the best and the brightest, the most motivated and capable individuals, are in leadership roles within the largest business units, or the nuclei. This is where the power and prestige is, where people manage large teams and substantial P&Ls and hold the most revered roles. Running the largest business unit is the place to be, the career aspiration of many highly talented and gifted individuals.

However, using our activity model, these superstars are primarily managing core and advancement activities. These business units typically show single-digit growth and are not going to add substantially to incremental shareholder value of the organization. Yes, these units are critical because they drive the value of the whole company, and even the slightest slip-up here equates to a misstep in the entire organization. But the plan and outlook for these units has largely been decided and is known across the company, and, at the risk of oversimplification, the leader's job is primarily to execute the plan and keep the ship running. Since the core and advancement activities that make up the bulk of work in these units have defined tools and approaches, the playbook is clear. Consequently, the set of executives who can effectively manage these business units may be larger than expected and extend beyond the select few managers who are considered the best and brightest.

Since the next generation of value creation is going to come from reframing and experiential activities, the question leaders must address is: Should the staffing model be reexamined so that the most-gifted talent is focused on activities that drive new value instead of the process of running the large and stable business units? Reframing and experiential activities are more nebulous and require creativity and the ability to deal with ambiguity. However, if the future of a company is defined by its ability to innovate, it is essential to staff these activities with the best employees and provide them with the right tools and knowledge for creating innovations. Additionally, these roles need to be viewed as being on par with any other role within the company, even though the number of dollars and people in these units aren't as large as the more established ones.

Similarly, rewards need to be reconsidered in an innovation biome. Creating a billion dollars of incremental value at a startup generates great wealth for the entrepreneurs who are the forces behind it. Creating a billion dollars of incremental value within a large corporation may bring about a handsome reward, but it is nowhere near the same level as at a startup. Clearly, the two settings have many differences and risk profiles, but if corporations don't want to lose their greatest value creators, the rewards system needs to be realigned so that internal innovators and entrepreneurs share far more in the benefits they helped create. The rewards for success need to match the value created, and a promotion or a generous annual bonus simply does not incentivize extreme value creation. Why not pay someone $20 million or more if they have developed a billion dollars of incremental value? This is an issue the leadership of an organization must tackle if there is a desire to create a new generation of value.

Worse yet, in many companies rewards are often tied to functional success, such as the successful achievement of tasks, and not to the market success of an initiative. A company may end up launching a new product that no one buys, but if it is done on time and under budget, the team is rewarded for doing their job well. These rewards are clearly for naught, as the entire initiative has failed.

Companies need to tie rewards for innovation with business outcomes and not task completion. One consideration could be a phantom stock or an agreement that the team responsible for building an innovation shares in the value creation through an approved mechanism. For example, the new innovation unit could be independently valued by an appraiser, and the team responsible for creating that value gets an agreed-upon percentage as a cash payment.

Issuance of phantom stock is simply one consideration, and there are several mechanisms that can be deployed to reward the generation of new value. The main point, however, is that rewards are often mismatched with results, which could be one reason why many of the most entrepreneurial people leave to start their own enterprises. If a corporate biome is designed to offer a better chance of innovation success than a startup, and employees understand the rewards of innovation and value creation, then entrepreneurs will have less reason to leave their jobs and create their own companies.

## Failure

New-value creation is a leap of faith, and a high degree of failure is expected. If you study the most innovative companies you can think of, you will find that they have had more failures than successes, more misses than hits. How you deal with failure is the hallmark of an innovation biome. No one knows beforehand what will work or be successful, so you need to expose yourself and your customers to a breadth of ideas and solutions. The business model of an innovation is uncertain, and while we might attempt to reduce this uncertainty through the development of experience deltas and other practices discussed in this book, innovation needs to run freely and with flexibility. Companies should not assume they know whether an innovation will work, how it will be used, who exactly will use it, or how it will be monetized. All of these variables need to be fluid, and the organization must be ready for change. Rigidity in any of these aspects is the antithesis to value creation.

Whether you are an individual or a corporation, innovation takes practice, and you are likely to have misses—far more misses than you anticipate. Here, the apocryphal quote from Thomas Edison is pertinent: "I have not failed 10,000 times. I have successfully found 10,000 ways that will not work." Every great innovator has a string of failures behind them. They had to fail, otherwise they would have missed out on the successes. As Thomas J. Watson is said to have pointed out, "If you want to increase your success rate, double your failure rate."

Failure is uncomfortable, but it is necessary if you are in the business of creating new value. Cerebrally we understand that we should encourage failure and even celebrate learn-fast, fail-fast methodologies. But practically it is hard to reward failure. If failure is rewarded, aren't we creating a culture of mediocrity rather than preeminence? Failure is not necessarily bad per se, but an innovation biome should be designed to maximize the odds of success, reduce the number of failures, and teach people valuable lessons from the missteps.

To do this, we must first do away with practices that are likely to generate a high rate of failure. For example, we need to think carefully about some traditional innovation methods in vogue today at many companies, such as setting up group brainstorming sessions to develop ideas that are rapidly prototyped and sent up the management chain for approval. We have already examined in earlier chapters why this approach is fraught with risks and has a higher chance of failure than using a more structured approach.

The way to determine whether an innovation will be successful is to first examine whether it has a positive experience delta (whether it is a marked improvement from current customer experiences). If we can see the positive impact an offering makes on an experience journey, then we know we have something on our hands that could potentially be valuable. If an innovation is unable to positively impact an experience journey, then it should be considered a no-go. The experience delta becomes the currency to decide whether to invest in an innovation or not.

Using the experience journey as a barometer reduces some of the subjectivity of the go/no-go decision. Although approving the resources for a new development is ultimately an individual manager's decision, the experience delta is a tool that can reduce the chance of failure. Using the experience delta as a lens for evaluating an innovation replaces opinions with something that can be used consistently.

Once an innovation decision is made and the development has started, there are two possible types of failures. The first is that the product or offering never gets built due to a technical inability to develop it, and the second is that the offering gets built but does not generate market success. Since we want to learn from failures, in each case there needs to be a structured postmortem analysis of why the innovation failed. If there is no appropriate examination of why things did not go as planned, then failure gets accepted naturally and becomes ingrained in the psyche of the organization—a condition we want to avoid.

If the failure happened because you couldn't build the product as originally envisioned, don't give up right away. In many cases persistence pays off. Gather a cross-functional set of people from multiple and disparate disciplines and discuss the matter. These individuals will apply a different lens to the problem. As we have seen, breakthroughs happen during such discussions, where multiple perspectives are shared. Or share the dead end with a larger community (internal or external to your organization) that can help develop a solution. Sometimes, despite your best efforts, a dead end simply can't be overcome, and you must make the decision to pull the plug on the innovation. Remember that just because a problem is unsolvable today does not mean it will never be solved. Keep the idea alive through documentation of the scenario. As other developments occur or different people get engaged in the work, old ideas get a new life. As we have discussed, always keep looking at the cutting-room floor for ideas that did not work at a specific point in time; they may work later.

If the innovation gets built and fails in the marketplace, despite having a positive experience delta or a high relative advantage over the alternatives, the postmortem should be guided by the principles of innovation diffusion. Was there truly a substantial gain in the experience delta over alternatives, or did we perceive the experience delta incorrectly? Was there a substantial disadvantage associated with the enhanced experience delta (such as unacceptable side effects or other unintended consequences)? Or did something else prevent successful diffusion of the innovation, such as perceived advantage, ease of use, cost, availability, quality, importance of the benefit, lack of awareness or any number of reasons classified under the buckets of complexity, compatibility, trialability, and observability.

The rate and acceptability of innovation failure vary with type of innovation activity. Using the CARE model presented earlier, advancement activities (incremental innovation) should have a lower failure rate than reframing and experiential activities. Advancement activities are driven by analyzing customers and testing market scenarios, and they tend to be more linear in nature. On the other hand, reframing and experiential activities are more undefined and attempt to create nonlinear value by breaking new ground through trial and error and untested theories. A higher failure rate from these activities should be expected.

Everyone talks about learning from failure. What exactly does that mean? Historically, companies have shown a low level of learning from failure and often repeat the same error. In innovation or new-value creation, we know we are embarking on a journey that is going to give us more misses than hits. We understand that we need to accept and learn from the misses. While we accept the failures, what exactly do we learn from them, and how can we apply that learning to future initiatives? Do we even have a strategy for failure analysis? A general practice is to have the initiative leader prepare a brief report or account documenting why something did not work as planned. And in most cases, this is sufficient because no one wants to relive failures, especially when the next big thing is waiting for our attention.

We can only learn from failure if we respect it enough to accept, analyze, understand, document, and reference it in the future. The first step in this process is recognizing failure when it surfaces early. If we know something is not going to work, we need to pull the plug and not mask failure as a work in progress. Then we need a non-judgmental environment where it can be discussed openly. Managers understandably do not like to talk about failure, but it is critical. We need to use structured postmortems to understand why an innovation did not work. Cross-functional teams without a vested interest are best at having an open discussion on failure. It is important to document what happened so others do not encounter the same situation, and this is what we mean when we say, "learning from failure." I recommend having a failure portal or knowledge repository where the details of each innovation that failed (for any reason) are archived and available to others to learn from. This level of introspection will also make the innovator more likely to be successful in future endeavors.

While the reasons for failure can be many and may be within or outside your control, the main point of this discussion is that it is okay to fail for the right reasons. But if there truly is a desire to learn from failures, then there needs to be a methodology in place to make that knowledge accessible to other innovators within the company so each endeavor adds real value, even if its market value did not materialize.

## Innovation democratized

Innovation is not the domain of a single person or department. It is not the domain of the R&D group, the product development group, or senior executives. Innovation comes from everywhere. It comes from people who deal with customers every day and know how things can be improved. It comes from people who build and sell products, serve and support customers, or think of an unusual way to do things.

As we have seen in earlier chapters, innovation does not only come from creative people; in fact, science has shown that everyone can be creative and that the left brain/right brain distinctions are a myth.[49] All sides of the brain are used all the time. Innovation comes from filling a need that may be stated or implicit. It can happen anywhere and at any time.

Every great development truly takes a village. And everyone can innovate. There are so many activities involved in getting a great new product to customers that everyone has an opportunity to do something innovative in the process. If you are not working on a product, you can still be innovative in sales, partnerships, marketing, distribution, packaging, or anything else. Reportedly the packaging of the iPhone (the box it comes in) is an innovation that is patented, with seventeen designers listed on the patent. The box is not treated simply as packaging that will be discarded; it is the first interaction a customer has with the product. It is considered

---

49  NeuroscienceNews.com, "Researchers Debunk Myth of 'Right-Brained' and 'Left-Brained' Personality Traits" (August 14, 2013), http://neurosciencenews.com/neuroimaging-left-right-brain-personality-trait-370/.

an important part of the experience that sets the tone for how the customer perceives the product.

An innovation biome encourages everybody in every department to be innovative. For the biome to result in breakthroughs, everybody needs to believe they are innovative. For example, I am still in a bit of disbelief that I am sitting here writing a book. I have to constantly remind myself that I have a book in me. And if you have this book and have reached this point, then I have made an impact. Everybody can make the same impact by believing they are innovative. Ultimately, innovation is simply driven by individuals who are willing to try something new.

Innovation is becoming increasingly democratized, by which I mean that it is more easily accessible to everyone than ever before. Since experiential innovation is about value creation through the connection of available components, the costs of innovation have come down considerably. Every component required for an innovation—whether it be materials, skills, software, know-how, manufacturing, or anything else—is usually available at a reasonable cost somewhere in the world. As a result, the ability to innovate is increasingly within everyone's reach, and organizations and individuals can take advantage of this opportunity to create new experiences quickly and inexpensively. The value is no longer in the components that are sourced; it is in the experiences created.

Organizations need to let innovation thrive in every department. To facilitate collaboration, many innovation software platforms can assist with idea development, exchange, flow, and refinement. As new concepts are generated, they can be socialized, or crowd sourced, to a large number of people for additional refinement. And since no one has a monopoly on great ideas, this is often a valuable way to enhance products.

Democratized innovation can also involve going outside the boundaries of an organization by co-creating with customers, suppliers, or partners. This involves openly sharing internal developments and working collaboratively up and down the supplier chain to create more value in new offerings. The concept of democratized innovation rests on the notion that people with a diverse mix of skills, experiences, and motivations can collaborate to create far more value than is possible independently. Innovation through a triumvirate of suppliers, corporations, and leading users has a clear and positive impact on the value of new offerings and the adoption of an innovation.

# In Closing

**I hope you have enjoyed reading this book** and find the lessons valuable. I do want to stress that building and bringing to market great, world-altering creations are within the abilities of almost everyone. This book is a labor of love and simply designed to bring together the key components of the innovation process with the current thinking and science behind each area. I believe you can create an innovation biome by applying the principles presented in this book, and I wish you all the best in your innovation journey.

I would love to hear from my readers. If you have any comments about the book, or if you would like to share your thoughts, learn more about the concepts presented here, or simply discuss how innovation can be advanced, please email me at kumar@kumarmehta.com.

# Index

*Note:* The "t" refers to table on the referenced page; the "n" refers to a footnote. On pages where two footnotes are references, the number of the footnote follows the "n."

# About the Author

**Dr. Kumar Mehta is an expert in innovation** science and dedicated to providing knowledge to help accelerate the rate of innovation across the globe. Kumar has been studying innovation before it became a buzzword, basing his 1990 dissertation on how groundbreaking ideas and technologies spread. Since then he has used his knowledge to create the conditions for innovative thought throughout his tenure in a large corporation as well as in building out imaginative and forward-thinking companies.

Kumar has been the CEO of a successful enterprise that employs over 1,200 professionals worldwide. Kumar has also spent over thirteen years at Microsoft honing his skills in innovation, data analytics, research, and business strategy. He frequently speaks around the world on these topics.

Kumar is passionate about education and serves on the board for the Committee for Children, a global nonprofit dedicated to fostering the safety and well-being of children through social-emotional learning and development.

Kumar also serves as a Senior Research Fellow at the Center for the Digital Future at the University of Southern California.

Kumar holds a PhD in pharmaceutical socioeconomics from the University of Iowa and lives in Seattle with his wife (his two young-adult children are on their own innovative journeys).